099

The Age of Rights

THE AGE OF RIGHTS

NORBERTO BOBBIO

Translated by Allan Cameron

Polity Press

English translation © Polity Press 1996
First published in Italy as *L'età dei diritti* © Guilio Einaudi 1990

This translation first published in 1996 by Polity Press in association with
Blackwell Publishers Ltd.

Reprinted 2005

2 4 6 8 10 7 5 3 1

Polity Press
65 Bridge Street
Cambridge CB2 1UR, UK

Polity Press
350 Main Street
Malden, MA 02148, USA

ISBN 0-7456-13845
ISBN 0-7456-15953 (pbk)

A CIP catalogue record for this book is available from the British Library
and the Library of Congress.

Typeset in on pt Palatino 10.5/12.5 pt
by Pure Tech India Ltd., Pondicherry.
Printed and bound in Great Britain by Marston Book Services Limited, Oxford

This book is printed on acid-free paper.

For further information on Polity, visit our website: www.polity.co.uk

Contents

Preface to the English Edition

I compiled this collection of articles on human rights on the suggestion and with the assistance of Luigi Bonanate and Michelangelo Bovero. I have written on this subject over a period of many years, and believe these to be the most important of my essays. The whole question is closely related to the issues of peace and democracy, to which I have devoted the bulk of my political writings. The recognition and protection of human rights are the foundations of modern democratic constitutions. Peace is, in turn, the precondition for the recognition and effective protection of human rights within individual states and within the international system. Equally, the democratization of the international system, which is the only way to achieve the ideal of 'perpetual peace' in the sense that Kant attributed to the expression, cannot move ahead without the gradual extension of this recognition and protection of human rights at a supranational level. Human rights, democracy and peace are the three essential components of the same historic movement: if human rights are not recognized and protected, there is no democracy, and without democracy, the minimal conditions for a peaceful resolution of conflicts do not exist. In other words, democracy is a society of citizens, and subjects become citizens when they are recognized as having certain fundamental rights. There will be stable peace, a peace which does not have war as its alternative, only when there are citizens not of this or that particular state, but of the world.

I first wrote on this subject in 1951, following a lecture on the Universal Declaration of Human Rights held in Turin on 4 May, at the invitation of the officers' training school.[1] On rereading it after all these years, I find that it contains, albeit in outline only, three theories which I have always continued to hold:

1 Natural rights are historic rights.
2 They came into existence at the beginning of the modern era, together with an individualistic perception of society.
3 They are one of the principal indicators of progress.

The first essay in this collection was one of the introductory lectures to a conference discussing the foundations of human rights held in L'Aquila in September 1964, and organized by the International Institute of Philosophy under the chairmanship of Guido Calogero (the other lecture was given by Perelman). The essay confirmed and analysed the historicist theory, which is my basis for disputing not only the legitimacy but also the practicality of the quest for an absolute principle.

This is followed by 'Human Rights Now and in the Future', the text for a lecture I gave in Turin in December of 1967 for the national conference on human rights held by the Società Italiana per l'Organizzazione Internazionale, on the twentieth anniversary of the Universal Declaration. Here, I illustrate the major developments in the history of human rights, from their proclamation to their implementation, and from their implementation within individual states to their implementation within the international system, a process which has only just begun. I then take up the historicist theme, and base my argument on the further expansion of human rights.

The third essay, 'The Age of Rights', which gives its title to the whole collection, is a speech which I gave under another title at the University of Madrid in September 1987, at the invitation of Professor Gregorio Peces-Barba Martinez, the director of the Instituto de Derechos Humanos in Madrid. As on previous occasions, I take up the historical and also the philosophical significance of the reversal of the relationship between the state and the citizen, which typifies the formation of the modern state. The emphasis has moved from the duties incumbent on a subject to the rights a citizen can demand. Politics are no longer viewed primarily from the sovereign's point of view, but more from that of the citizen, which reflects the success of the individualistic concept of society over the traditional perception of it as an organic whole. For the first time, I demonstrated how the expansion of human rights occurred, moving from an abstraction of the individual, through a gradual differentiation, recognition and protection of needs and interests, to a more concrete concept.

I presented a further and for the moment final reformulation of the historicist arguments in my next essay 'Human Rights and Society', which I wrote as an introductory report for the international conference on 'The Sociology of Rights', held in Bologna at the end of May 1988. It discusses some general problems on the theory and history of human rights. I devote a few pages to the anguished theoretical debate on the concept of law applied to human rights, and then return to it a little later in the book.

Part II contains three lectures on human rights and the French Revolution. The first was given on 14 December 1988 in Rome for the inauguration of the new Library of the Chamber of Deputies at the invitation of the speaker, Nilde Jotti. I gave the second lecture in September of 1989 at the Fondazione Giorgio Cini in Venice, to open a course on the French Revolution, and the third lecture when I was awarded an honorary degree at Bologna University on 6 April 1989. This last lecture took Kant's philosophical works on law and history as its starting point, and finished by emphasizing Kant's theory of a universal law of nature as the conclusion to the debate on human rights so far, but also leading towards further considerations.[2]

Part III contains two pieces on the death penalty. The first was written for the Fourth National AGM of Amnesty International in Rimini in April of 1981, and the second for the international conference on 'The Death Penalty in the World', held in Bologna in October of 1982.[3]

These writings discuss problems which are both historical and theoretical. I argue that historically the affirmation of human rights derives from a radical inversion of the political relationship between the state and the citizen, or the sovereign and the subject. This relationship is increasingly seen in terms of the rights of citizens who are no longer merely subjects, while the sovereign's powers decline in line with a more individualistic concept of society.[4] According to this new perception, in order to understand society one has to start from its base and the individuals that make it up. This runs counter to the traditional organic concept of society as a whole which takes priority over its individual members. The inverted perspective was principally induced by the religious wars at the beginning of the modern era, and has since become an irreversible process. That experience gave rise to the right to resist oppression, which presupposes a primary and more substantial right: the right of each individual not to be oppressed and to enjoy a few fundamental liberties. These liberties are fundamental because they are natural, and they are natural because they do not depend on the consent of the sovereign. The most fundamental of all these liberties is religious freedom.

This reversal is closely connected to the affirmation of what I have defined as the natural law model, as opposed to its eternal adversary, the Aristotelian model, which is always reappearing and has never quite been defeated.[5] Although there have been many setbacks, the individualistic concept of society has made slow but steady progress from the recognition of a citizen's rights within a single state to the recognition of a citizen's rights within the world, as was first announced in the Universal Declaration of Human Rights. The question has moved from the realm of each state's individual law, through laws established between states, towards a cosmopolitan right, to use Kant's expression (his contribution to legal theory has not yet been fully recognized).

An authoritative internationalist in a recent work on human rights wrote: 'The Declaration has favoured the emergence of the individual in an arena which was previously reserved exclusively for heads of state, even though this presence is still weak, tenuous and hesitant. It has started an irreversible process, which we should all see as a cause for celebration.'[6]

My theoretical approach has always been and continues to be, in the light of new arguments, that human rights however fundamental are historical rights and therefore arise from specific conditions characterized by the embattled defence of new freedoms against old powers. They are established gradually, not all at the same time, and not for ever.[7] It would appear that philosophers are asked to pass sentence on the fundamental nature of human rights, and even to demonstrate that they are absolute, inevitable and incontrovertible, but the question should not be posed in these terms.[8] Religious freedom resulted from the religious wars, civil liberties from the parliamentarian struggles against absolutism, and political and social freedoms from the birth, growth and experience of movements representing workers, landless peasants and smallholders. The poor demand from the authorities not only recognition of personal freedom and negative freedoms, but also protection against unemployment, basic education to overcome illiteracy, and gradually further forms of welfare for sickness and old age – all needs which the wealthy can provide for themselves.

Next to this so-called second generation of rights which concern social questions, there is now emerging a third generation of rights which is still too vague and heterogeneous for an exact definition.[9] The most important of these is being demanded by the ecological movements: the right to live in an unpolluted environment. But there are already signs of what I could only call the fourth generation of rights, which concern the increasingly disturbing results of biological research and the ability to manipulate an individual's genetic identity.[10] It is a question of the limits which can be placed on this imminent future manipulation, as it moves from the realm of probability into that of reality. This is yet another proof, if such were needed, that rights do not originate together. They come into existence, when their existence is either essential or possible. They arise from the increasing power of one man over another, the inevitable consequence of technical progress which increases man's ability to dominate nature and other men. This progress either creates new threats to individual freedom, or allows new remedies for mass deprivation. The threats are countered with demands for limitations on power, and the remedies require protective intervention by that same power. The former relate to the rights to enjoy freedoms, or to non-intervention by the state, and the latter relate to social rights, or rights to positive intervention by the state. Although the demands for rights can be categorized chronologically in different stages or

generations, they have only two types of relationship to the constituted powers: they either restrict their ability to do harm or
encourage their ability to do good. Rights of the third and fourth
generation can be of either type.

In one of my essays, 'Human Rights and Society', (this volume,
chapter 4), I demonstrate the proliferation of demands for new
forms of recognition and protection, as the considerations of abstract man developed into those of man in the various stages of
life, and this proliferation has met with some opposition. The
third-generation rights, such as the right to live in an unpolluted
environment, would have been unimaginable when the second-
generation rights were being put forward, just as second-genera-
tion rights like the right to education and welfare would have
been inconceivable when the first seventeenth-century declarations were made. Specific demands are created in response to
specific needs. New needs are created by changes in social conditions, and when technical developments make it possible to satisfy them. Talk of natural, fundamental, inalienable or inviolable
rights may represent a persuasive formula to back a demand in a
political publication, but it has no theoretical value, and is therefore completely irrelevant to human rights theory.

The debate over the meaning of 'rights' in the expression
'human rights' has been protracted and confused.[11] Confusion has
been further increased by more frequent links between Anglo-
Saxon lawyers and those of a continental tradition and culture.
They often use different words to say the same things, but occasionally think they are saying different things when they are using
the same words. Continental legal terminology has traditionally
distinguished between 'natural rights' and 'positive rights'. Britain and the United States – principally under the influence of
Dworkin, I believe – have provided us with the distinction between 'moral rights' and 'legal rights', which cannot be translated
into Italian and, what is more, is incomprehensible to a tradition
in which law and morality are two clearly distinct spheres of
practical life. In Italian the expressions 'legal rights' or 'juridical
rights' sound tautological, while the expression 'moral rights'
sounds contradictory. I have no doubt that a French jurist would
be equally reluctant to speak of *droits moraux* and a German of
moralische Rechte. The only way to avoid giving up all hope of

understanding one another is to consider to what extent the two distinctions are comparable. Thus 'moral rights' as against 'legal rights' belongs to the same domain as 'natural rights' as against 'positive rights'. In both cases, it is a distinction between two different normative systems, while the criterion for the distinction differs. The distinction between 'moral rights' and 'legal rights' is based on their principles, and the distinction between 'moral rights' and 'legal rights' is based on their origins. In all four cases, however, the word 'right' in the sense of a subjective right (a superfluous specification in English, because 'right' can only mean 'subjective right'), refers to a normative system, whether it is called 'moral', 'natural', 'legal' or 'positive'. Just as natural rights would be inconceivable without a system of natural laws, it would be equally impossible to understand 'moral rights' without reference to a set or system of laws which one could define as moral, even though it is never clear what their actual status is (the status of natural laws is equally unclear).

I agree with those who claim that 'rights' are a deontic entity, which have a precise meaning only in normative language. There is no right without obligation, and there is neither right nor obligation without behavioural norms. The uncommon expression 'moral rights' becomes less irksome if it is related to the very common expression 'moral obligations'. The old objection that rights cannot be given without obligations, but obligations can be imposed without rights, arises from a confusion between two different normative systems. Of course one cannot demand that each moral obligation has a corresponding legal right, because a moral right can only correspond to a moral obligation. The much-quoted but misleading example that the moral obligation to give alms does not establish the right to beg, only demonstrates that a moral obligation does not establish a legal obligation.

The same could perhaps be said of moral rights. What could the expression 'moral right' mean if not a right corresponding to a moral obligation? What jurists might consider to be a *jus imperfectum* could be *jus perfectum* from a moral point of view. I know very well that a tradition going back over a thousand years has accustomed us to a use of the term *jus* which is restricted to a normative system which is more binding than all the other moral and social systems, but when the notion of 'moral right' is introduced, the corresponding 'moral obligation' is necessarily introduced along with it. If I have a moral right in relation to someone, this means that someone has a moral obligation to me. Moral language is not obliged to use the deontic categories of right and obligation, which are more appropriate to legal language, but from the moment it does use them, the establishment of a right implies the affirmation of an obligation, and vice versa. Whether the establishment of a right precedes an obligation or follows it, is a matter of pure historical accident. For example, there are various debates today about our current obligations to future generations, but the question could be considered from the standpoint of future generations' rights from us. As far as the substance of the problem is concerned, it is a matter of complete indifference whether you start from the obligation of the former or the rights of the latter. Does posterity have rights in relation to us, because we have obligations to them, or vice versa? If you pose the question in these terms, it is immediately clear that the logic of the terminology demonstrates the complete absence of any problem.

In spite of countless attempts to come up with a definitive analysis, the terminology for rights remains very ambiguous, lacking in rigour, and is often used rhetorically. There is no rule against using the same term for rights which have only been proclaimed, however renowned the declaration, as for rights actually protected by a judicial system founded on constitutional principles with impartial judges whose decisions have various forms of executive power. There is, however, a great deal of difference between the two! Even the greater part of the social rights, the so-called rights of the second generation, which exhibit such lofty intentions in national and international declarations, have remained dead letters, and this is all the more true of the third- and fourth-generation rights. The only thing we can establish so far is that they are the expressions of ideals aspired to, and the title of 'rights' serves only to give them an aura of nobility. To proclaim the right of all people to live in an environment free from pollution in whatever part of the world they live (human rights are by their very nature universal) does not mean anything other than an aspiration that future legislation will impose limitations on the use of pollutants. It is one thing to proclaim this right, and entirely another to enjoy its fruits. The language used in connection with rights undoubtedly has a considerable practical application, which is to reinforce the demands by movements on behalf of themselves and others for the satisfaction of new material and moral needs, but becomes misleading if it obscures the difference between a right which is being campaigned for and a right which is recognized and protected. Otherwise, one could not explain the contradiction between those writings which celebrate this age of rights,[12] and those which demonstrate the mass of people to be 'without rights'.[13] The former only discuss the rights proclaimed in international courts and conferences, and the latter discuss the rights which the great majority of humankind do not enjoy *de facto* (even though they are solemnly and repeatedly proclaimed).

Norberto Bobbio
Turin, October 1990

Notes

1 'La Dichiarazione universale dei diritti dell'uomo', in *La Dichiarazione universale dei diritti dell'uomo* (Turin: Arti Grafiche Plinio Castello, 1951), pp. 53–70. I had already addressed this question briefly in the preface to the Italian translation of Georges Gurvitch's *La Dichiarazione dei diritti sociali* (Milan: Edizioni di Comunità, 1949), pp. 13–27.

2 See also my introduction to I. Kant, *Per la pace perpetua*, ed. N. Merker (Rome: Editori Riuniti, 1985), pp. vii–xxi.

3 Some of my other writings on human rights are to be found in *Il terzo assente. Saggi e discorsi sulla pace e sulla guerra*, ed. Pietro Polito (Milan: Edizioni Sonda, 1989). However, neither *Il terzo assente* nor this present volume contain 'Il preambolo della Convenzione europea dei diritti dell 'uomo', *Rivista di diritto internazionale*, vol. LVII (1973), pp. 437–55, 'Vi sono diritti fondamentali?', *Rivista di filosofia*, vol. LXXI, no. 18 (1980), pp. 460–4, 'Diritti dell'uomo e diritti del cittadino nel secolo XIX in Europa', in *Grundrechte im 19. Jahrhundert* (Frankfurt: P. Lang, 1982), pp. 11–15, and 'Dalla priorità dei doveri alla priorità dei diritti', *Mondoperaio*, vol. XLI, no. 3 (1988), pp. 57–60.

4 There is a vast amount of writing on this subject, but I would like to refer, here, to a little-known work: Celso Lafer, *A reconstruçao dos direitos humanos. Um diálogo con o pensamento de Hannah Arendt* (São Paolo:

Companhia das Letras, 1988), which contains some important pages on Individualism and its history, partly with reference to Arendt's thought.

5 I am referring particularly to my essay 'Il modello giusnaturalistico', in N. Bobbio and M. Bovero, *Società e stato nella filosofia politica moderna* (Milan: Il Saggiatore, 1979), pp. 17–109.

6 A. Cassese, *I diritti umani nel mondo contemporaneo* (Bari: Laterza, 1988), p. 143.

7 One of the central themes in a well-researched essay by G. Peces-Barba Martinez is that human rights are historic rights, which arose in the modern era from struggles against the absolute state: see G. Peces-Barba Matinez, 'Sobre el puesto de la historia en el concepto de los derechos fundamentales', in *Anuario de derechos humanos*, ed. Instituto de Derechos Humanos (Madrid: The Complutensian University, 1986–7), vol. IV, pp. 219–58. For the history of human rights in terms of their recognition, which is the only significant viewpoint, see G. Pugliese, 'Appunti per una storia della protezione dei diritti dell'uomo', *Rivista trimestrale di diritto e procura civile*, vol. XLIII, no. 3 (1989), pp. 619–59.

8 See *El fundamento de los derechos humanos*, ed. G. Peces-Barba Martinez (Madrid: Editorial Debate, 1989). This work summarizes the debate held in Madrid on 19–20 April 1998, and often refers to my position. It also contains an essay by the editor, 'Sobre el fundamento de los derechos humanos. Un problema de moral y derecho', pp. 265–77, which is the author's most recent expression of his ongoing reflections on human rights, which commenced with *Derechos fundamentales*, which was first published in 1976 and has been reprinted several times.

9 The concept of a third generation of rights has appeared in the growing body of writings on 'new rights'. In his article 'Sobre la evolución contemporánea de la teoria de los derechos de l'hombre', Jean Rivera lists some of these new rights as the rights to solidarity, and the rights to development, international peace, a safe environment and communication. Not surprisingly, the author then questions whether such a list can be considered rights in the strict sense, and not just simple aspirations or desires ('Corrientes y problemas en filosofia del derecho', *Anales de la cátedra Francisco Suarez*, 1985, no. 25, p. 193). Later, in his book which I have already referred to, he considers human rights of the third generation to be rights, not of individuals, but of groups of people, such as a family, a people, a nation, and humanity itself (p. 131). For the right to peace, see A. Ruiz Miguel, 'Tenemos derecho a la paz?', *Anuario de derechos humanos*, 3 (1984–5), pp. 387–434 (a publication edited by G. Peces-Barba Martinez for the Instituto de derechos humanos in Madrid), and by the same author, *La justicia de la guerra y de la paz* (Madrid: Centro de Estudios constitucionales, 1988), pp. 271ff. A.E. Perez has also written on the third generation of rights: 'Concepto y conceptión de los derechos humanos, *Cuadernos de*

filosofia del derecho, 1988, pp. 271ff. He lists the right to peace, consumers' rights, the quality of life and access to computerized information, and he relates their emergence to the development of new technologies.

10 There is already a considerable literature on this theme, especially in the Anglo-Saxon countries. It has been summarized by Bartha Maria Knoppers, 'L'integrità del patrimonio genetico: diritto soggettivo o diritto dell'umanità?', *Politica del diritto*, vol. XXXI, no. 2 (June 1990), pp. 341–61.

11 I took many suggestions for this argument from the debate on 'El concepto de derechos humanos' in *Cuadernos de filosofia del derecho*, no. 4, 1987, pp. 23–84, with various contributions on the basis of Francisco La Porta's report, and Eugenio Bulygin's conclusions 'Sobre el status ontológico de los derechos humanos', pp. 79–84. I find myself substantially in agreement with them. There has been considerable discussion over whether or not the concept of rights is to be interpreted as a normative concept, and whether 'moral rights' is an acceptable expression, and if so, how they can be defined. For a critique of the concept of 'moral right' and other considerations which I share, see R. Vernengo, 'Dos ensayos Sobre problemas de fundamentación de los derechos humanos', in *Cuadernos de investigaciones de l'Instituto de Investigaciones jurídicas y sociales Ambrogio L. Gioia* (Buenos Aires: Facultad de derecho y ciencias sociales, 1989), particularly the first essay: *Fundamentaciones morales de los derechos humanos*, pp. 4–29. See also Peces-Barba Marinez, 'Sobre el puesto . . .', p. 222. Recently there has been a debate on these topics in Italy as well; I refer particularly to F. Fagiani, 'Etica e teoria dei diritti' and L. Gianformaggio, 'Rapporto fra etica e diritti', both in *Teorie etiche contemporanee* (Turin: Bollati-Boringhieri, 1990), pp. 86–107 and pp. 149–61. For a more general view, see F. Viola, *Diritti dell'uomo, diritto naturale, etica contemporanea* (Turin: Giappichelli, 1989).

12 On the importance of the recognition of human rights in the current phase of human history, see the recent authoritative essay by Norbert Elias, 'Pianeta dei diritti', *Rinascita*, vol. I, no. 17 (June 1990).

13 See L. Bertozzi, 'Uomini senza diritti', *Rinascita*, vol. I, no. 27 (12 August 1990), pp. 72–4. Bertozzi, in the same journal, reports on the violations of human rights denounced by Amnesty International in its previous annual report. For research in Italy, see G. Ricordy, *Senza diritti. Storie dell'altra Italia* (Milan: Feltrinelli, 1990).

Note

Chapter 1, 'On the Fundamental Principles of Human Rights' ('Sul fondamento dei diritti dell'uomo'), was originally a paper given at a conference held in L'Aquila on 14–19 September 1964, and was published under the title 'L'Illusion du fondament absolu' in *Le Fondament des droits de l'homme* (Florence: La Nuova Italia, 1966), pp. 3–9. The Italian translation 'Sul fondamento dei diritti dell'uomo' appeared in *Rivista internazionale di filosofia del diritto*, vol. XLII (1965), pp. 302–9, and in *Il problema della guerra e le vie della pace* (Bologna: Il Mulino, 1979), pp. 119–30. Chapter 2, 'Human Rights Now and in the Future' ('Presente e avvenire dei diritti dell'uomo') was published in *La comunità internazionale*, vol. XXIII (1968), pp. 3–18, and later in *Il problema della guerra e le vie della pace*, pp. 131–57. It was translated into Castillian under the title 'Presente y porvenir de los derechos humanos' in *Anuario de derechos humanos* (Madrid: Complutensian University, 1982), pp. 7–28. Chapter 3, 'The Age of Rights' ('L'età dei diritti'), a lecture given in Madrid in September of 1987, was published in N. Bobbio, *Il terzo assente. Saggi e discorsi sulla pace e sulla guerra* (Turin: Edizioni Sonda, 1989), pp. 112–25, and with the title 'Derechos del hombre y filosofia de la historia' in *Anaurio de derechos humanos* (Madrid: Complutensian University, 1988–9), pp. 27–39. Chapter 4, 'Human Rights and Society' ('Diritti dell'uomo e società'), appeared in *Sociologia del diritto*, vol. XXVI (1989), pp. 15–27. Chapter 5, 'Human Rights Today' ('I diritti dell'uomo, oggi'), was an end-of-year address to the Accademia dei Lincei (14 June 1991), which was published in *Atti dell'Accademia Nazionale dei Lincei*, vol. CCCLXXXVIII, no. IX, series 2 (1991, pp. 55–64. Chapter 6, 'The French Revolution and Human Rights' (*La Rivoluzione francese e i diritti dell'uomo*), was published as pamphlet by the Chamber of Deputies in Rome in 1988, and then with the title 'La dichiarazione dei diritti dell'uomo' in *Nuova Antologia*, no. 2169 (January–March 1989, pp. 290–309. Chapter 7, 'The Legacy of the Great Revolution' ('L'eredità della grande Rivoluzione'), also appeared in *Nuova Antologia*, no. 2172 (October–December 1989, pp. 87–100, as did Chapter 8, 'Kant and the French Revolution' ('Kant e la Rivoluzione francese'), no. 2175 (July–September 1990, pp. 53–60. Chapter 9, 'Against the Death Penalty' (*Contro la pena di morte*), was published as a pamphlet by the Italian section of Amnesty International (Bologna: Tipostampa bolognese, 1981), while Chapter 10, 'The Current Debate on the Death Penalty' ('Il dibattito attuale sulla pena di morte'), was published in *La pena di morte nel mondo*, the proceedings of an international conference in Bologna, 28–30 October 1982 (Casale Monferrato: Marietti, 1983), pp. 15–32.

Part I

1 On the Fundamental Principles of Human Rights

1. I am going to discuss three topics in this essay: first, the nature of the problem we face over an absolute principle for human rights; second, whether an absolute principle is possible; and third, supposing it were possible, whether it would be desirable.

2. The question of a fundamental principle for a right has to be posed differently according to whether it is *a right which has been attained* or *a right which one aspires to attain*. In the first case, I would go and look through the positive legal code, which affects me as the possessor of rights and obligations, in search of a valid regulation which recognizes the right in question. In the second case, I would attempt to find good reasons for maintaining its legitimacy and persuading as many people as possible to acknowledge it, particularly those people who have the power directly or indirectly to put valid legislation on to the statute book.

In a debate such as this, which is for philosophers and not jurists, there can be little doubt that when we pose the question of the fundamental principle of human rights, we are referring to the second problem. In other words, it is not a question of positive rights, but rational or critical rights (or if you like, natural rights, but in a restricted meaning of the term, which is the only one I find acceptable). We are starting from the premise that human rights are something desirable, i.e. an objective worthy of pursuit, and in

spite of their desirability, they have not all been recognized everywhere and to the same degree. We wish for others to share our
decision, and are therefore motivated by the conviction that finding a fundamental principle to justify it would be an appropriate
method for obtaining wider recognition.

3.   The illusion in an absolute fundamental principle arises from
this belief that by dint of accumulating and assessing justifications
and arguments one after another, we shall finally come up with
the irrefutable argument, the one whose reasoning no one could
deny. The absolute principle is the undisputed principle in the
universe of our ideas, in the same way that absolute power is the
undisputed power in the universe of actions (think of Hobbes).
The mind inevitably bows to the undisputed principle, just as the
will bows to undisputed power. The ultimate principle cannot be
discussed further, just as ultimate power must be obeyed without
argument. Those who resist the former, put themselves outside
the community of reasonable people; and those who resist the
latter, puts themselves outside the community of the good and the
just.

For centuries this illusion was common among advocates of
natural law, who believed they had safeguarded certain rights
from any possible confutation by deducing them from human
nature (although the rights were not always the same). However,
human nature has proved to be a very shaky foundation on which
to build an absolute principle for incontrovertible rights. This is
not the place to repeat the countless criticisms which have been
made against the doctrine of natural rights, or to reveal yet again
the speciousness of arguments used to demonstrate their absolute
value. Suffice it to recall that many rights have been derived from
the generous and obliging nature of man, however varied their
character or however obscure (fundamental rights only in the eyes
of their champions). For instance, advocates of natural law argued
for a long time whether the most natural of three possible forms
of inheritance was for property to return to the community, to
pass from father to son, or to be freely disposed of by the propri-
etor (and which therefore was to be preferred in a system which
accepted as just everything that was founded on nature). The
argument could go on: all three solutions conform perfectly to
human nature, according to whether you consider man as a mem-

ber of a community on whom his life ultimately depends, as a *pater familias* whose natural instinct is to continue the species, or as a free and autonomous individual who is the only person responsible for his own actions and property.

Kant quite reasonably restricted the incontrovertible rights (which he called 'innate') to one: freedom. But what is freedom?

4. Today this illusion is no longer possible. Every attempt at an absolute principle has proved to be groundless. I can raise four objections to this illusion (and thus I move on to the second argument).

The first objection arises from the consideration that 'human rights' is a very vague expression. Have we ever attempted to define them, and if so, to what effect? Most of the definitions are pure tautology: 'The rights of man are those which are due to a man in as much as he is a man'. Sometimes they tell us something about the desired or proposed status of these rights, and nothing about their content: 'The rights of man are those which belong or should belong to all men, and of which he should not be deprived'. Finally, whenever there is some reference to content, it is impossible to avoid the introduction of terms requiring value judgements: 'Human rights are those whose recognition is a necessary condition for the improvement of humanity or the development of civilization, etc.' This leads to another problem: such terms can be interpreted in different ways according to the ideology of the interpreter. The improvement of humanity and the development of civilization are themselves the subject of passionate and irresolvable debates. Agreement is generally achieved by the disputants making reciprocal concessions until they can arrive at some general formula which is just as vague as the previous two definitions. However, disagreements which have been papered over soon reappear, whenever one attempts to put a purely verbal statement into practice.

The only thing we know about fundamental rights is that they are necessary for the achievement of final values, and they are therefore an appeal to those final values. But final values themselves cannot be justified but only premised: that which is final is, by its very nature, without foundation. Moreover, final values are antinomical, and cannot all be accomplished universally at the same time. It is necessary for both parties to make concessions in order to achieve them, and the concessions required for this process of conciliation involve personal preferences, political choices and ideological orientations. All three of these types of definition do not therefore allow us to develop a well-defined category of human rights. One wonders how the question of fundamental principles for human rights, whether absolute or not, can be addressed when it is not possible to formulate a precise concept.

5. Secondly, human rights constitute a variable category as is adequately demonstrated by the history of the last few centuries. The list of human rights has been modified and continues to be modified in changing historical circumstances: the requirements and interests of the ruling classes, the available means for their enactment, technological developments, etc. Rights, which were declared absolute at the end of the eighteenth century, such as the *sacre et inviolable* right of ownership, have now been subjected to radical restrictions in contemporary declarations, while prominence is now given to rights, such as social rights, which in the seventeenth century did not even get a mention. It is not difficult to foresee that new demands will emerge which at the moment we can only catch a glimpse of, such as the right not to carry arms against one's wishes or the right to respect the lives of animals and not just humans. Thus rights are not fundamental by their nature. That which appears to be fundamental in a given historical era or civilization, is not fundamental in other eras or civilizations.

It is difficult to see how a fundamental principle can be attributed to rights which are historically relative. But we should not be frightened of relativism. The evident plurality of religious and moral perceptions is a historical fact, and these too are subject to change. The relativism which derives from this pluralism is itself relative. It is precisely this pluralism which constitutes the most powerful argument in favour of some of the most significant human rights, such as religious freedom and freedom of thought in general. If we were not convinced of the irreducible plurality of teleological concepts, but instead believed that religious, ethical and political declarations could be demonstrated by theorems (as advocates of natural law illuded themselves – Hobbes, for example, called natural laws 'theorems'), then the right to religious freedom or the freedom of political thought would lose their reason for existence, or at the very least would acquire a different meaning: they would no longer be the right to follow one's own personal religion or to express one's own political opinion, but would become the right not to be deviated by force from the pursuit of the one true religion or the single political good. It is worth noting the profound difference between the right to religious freedom and the right to scientific freedom. Religious freedom is the right to profess any religion or no religion at all. Scientific freedom is not the right to profess any scientific truth or none at all, but is essentially the right to pursue scientific research unimpeded.

6. Apart from being ill-defined (§ 4) and variable (§ 5), the category of human rights is also heterogeneous. The same declaration can include very different kinds of demand and, what is worse, demands which are incompatible. The arguments used for some of the demands are not therefore valid for others. In such a case, we should not be talking of the principle but the principles of human rights, of different principles according to which right we are arguing for.

As has been observed on several occasions, the 'status' of human rights varies. There are some which are valid in every situation and concern all human beings without distinction, such as the right not be enslaved or not to be tortured. No limitations are requested for such rights either on the basis of exceptional circumstances or in relation to this or that category of humankind, which may be extremely restricted. These rights are privileged, because they cannot be impinged upon by any other rights, however fundamental, and do not involve a choice in given situations or in relation to particular categories.

It is not possible to assert a new right in favour of one group of persons without suppressing a former right enjoyed by another group of persons. The recognition of the right not to be enslaved implies the elimination of the right to own slaves; the recognition of the right not to be tortured implies the suppression of the right to torture. In these cases, the choice seems easy and self-evident, so we would be surprised if anyone asked us to justify them (we consider morally self-evident that which does not have to be justified).

In the majority of cases, however, the choice is doubtful and needs to be demonstrated, because both the right which is being asserted and the right which is being suppressed have arguments in their favour. In Italy, for example, there is a demand for the abolition of censorship on films shown in cinemas. The choice is simple: you put the artist's freedom on one scale and on the other scale the freedom of government bodies, which are generally incompetent and mean-minded, to suffocate the artist. But the problem becomes more difficult if you oppose the film producer's right of expression to the public's right not to be shocked, offended or provoked. The problem is resolved by introducing limitations on both rights so that each is safeguarded to some extent. To continue our example of film censorship, our constitution provides for the limit of good taste.

It would appear, therefore, that rights with such different areas of pertinence cannot have the same foundation, and above all that rights of the second type, which may well be fundamental but are subject to restrictions cannot have an absolute foundation, because this would invalidate the restriction.

7. One must distinguish between the previously discussed situation of a clash between the fundamental right of one category of persons and the equally fundamental right of another category, and a situation which even more seriously undermines the search for an absolute principle: the situation which involves a contradiction between the rights claimed by the same group of persons. All the recent declarations of human rights include not only the traditional individual rights or 'freedoms', but also the so-called social rights or 'powers'. The former require purely negative obligations from others (including public bodies), and for those others to refrain from certain forms of behaviour, while the latter can be achieved only if a certain number of positive obligations are imposed on others (including public bodies). They are antinomical in the sense that they cannot both be developed at the same time: the comprehensive implementation of one set of rights precludes the comprehensive implementation of the other set. The greater the powers of each individual, the lesser his on her freedoms. These are two legal situations so different that the arguments used to uphold the former are worthless for the latter. The two principle arguments for introducing the most fundamental freedoms are:

1 the impossibility of establishing teleological beliefs;
2 the belief that the greater the liberty an individual can enjoy, the more he or she can progress morally and promote the material progress of society.

Well, the first of these arguments is irrelevant to the demands for new powers, and the second has proven to be historically incorrect.

Two fundamental but contradictory rights cannot have a single absolute principle which makes them both irrefutable and irresistible. It is worth recalling here that the illusion of an absolute principle for some established rights has been an obstacle to the introduction of new rights which were wholly or partially incompatible. Consider, for instance, the obstacles posed to the progress of social legislation by the theory of natural law which upheld the absolute principle of property. For almost a hundred years, opposition to the introduction of social rights was carried out in the name of the absolute principle of libertarian rights. The absolute principle is not only an illusion; on occasions it is also a pretext for defending conservative positions.

8. So far, I have put forward arguments to explain the futility of searching for an absolute principle for human rights. But there is another aspect which emerges from the previous considerations, and leads me to the third question I posed at the beginning. It is the matter of ascertaining whether the successful discovery of a fundamental principle would achieve the hoped-for result of a speedier and more effective recognition and implementation of human rights. The debate concerns the second dogma of ethical rationalism and illusion of natural law which maintains not only that final values can be demonstrated by theorems, but that it is sufficient to demonstrate them (to prove them irrefutable and indisputable) in order to ensure their implementation. Apart from the dogma of the demonstrability of final values whose lack of foundation I have been attempting to prove in the previous paragraphs, ethical rationalism in its more extreme and old-fashioned formulations also claims that the rational demonstration of a value is not only a necessary condition for its implementation, but is sufficient by itself. The first dogma presumes the *power* of reason, the second presumes its *primacy*.

History disproves this second dogma of ethical rationalism and natural law, which is its most conspicuous historical expression. I have three arguments on this point.

Firstly, it cannot be said that human rights were more respected during the period in which the learned were in agreement that they had found the irrefutable argument for their defence, i.e. the absolute principle that they could be derived from human nature or the essence of humanity. Secondly, the greater part of existing governments have proclaimed by mutual agreement a Universal Declaration of Human Rights over the last few decades, in spite of collapse in the plausibility of fundamental principles. As a consequence of this declaration, the problem of principles has lost much of its interest. If the majority of existing governments have agreed to a common declaration, it is a sign that they had good reasons for doing so. The question now is not how to establish arguments, or a single all-embracing argument as the born-again believers in natural law would have it, but to create the conditions for a wider and more rigorous implementation of the rights proclaimed. Clearly one has to believe that the implementation of human rights is a desirable end if one is to work for these conditions, but this conviction is not enough in itself to create them. Many of these conditions (and here I move on to the third argument) do not depend upon the good will of governments, and still less upon the clever arguments used to demonstrate the absolute good of particular rights. For example, it is only the industrial transformation of a country which makes it possible to protect the rights connected with labour relations. It should be remembered that the strongest argument presented by reactionaries in all countries against human rights, and particularly against social rights, is not their lack of foundation, but their infeasibility. When it comes to proclaiming them, it is relatively easy to reach an agreement, but when it comes to their implementation, reservations and hostilities start to appear.

The fundamental problem concerning human rights today is not so much how to justify them, but how to protect them. This problem is political, not philosophical.

9. There can be no denying that there has been a collapse in the influence of fundamental principles, but we must not attempt to overcome this reality by attempting to find another absolute prin-

ciple to replace the one lost. Our task today is much more modest, but also more difficult. We do not have to find the absolute principle, a sublime but desperate undertaking, but rather *the various possible principles* for each particular circumstance. However, even this study of possible principles (a legitimate undertaking which unlike the other is not doomed to failure) will not have any historical importance if it is not accompanied by the study of the conditions, the means and the situations in which a given right can be implemented. This research is the task of historians and social scientists. The philosophical problem of human rights cannot be dissociated from the study of the historical, social, economic and psychological problems inherent in their implementation. The problem of ends is a problem of the means, and this signifies that the philosopher is no longer alone. The philosopher who insists on staying alone is condemning philosophy to a sterile role. This crisis of belief in principles is also an aspect of the crisis in philosophy.

2 Human Rights Now and in the Future

Three years ago at the conference organized by the Institut International de Philosophie on 'The Principle of Human Rights', I stated categorically at the end of my paper[1] that the critical problem facing our times was not one of finding fundamental principles for human rights, but that of protecting them. Since then I have had no cause to change my mind. My assertion might have had a polemical intention, when directed at an audience of philosophers, but when I repeated it to the mainly legal conference organized by the Italian Consultative Committee on Human Rights,[2] it acted as the almost essential introduction.

The problem we are faced with is not, in fact, philosophical but legal and, in a wider sense, political. It is not a matter of knowing which and how many of these rights there are, what their nature is and on what foundation they are based, whether they are natural or historical, absolute or relative; it is a question of finding the surest method for guaranteeing rights, and preventing their continuing violation in spite of all the solemn declarations. When the last session of the General Assembly ratified the decision made in the previous session, that the International Conference on Human Rights should take place in Teheran in the spring of 1968, it expressed its hope that the conference would make 'a considerable step forward in the action being taken to encourage and extend the *respect* for human rights and fundamental liberties'.[3] It is understood that the need 'to respect' human rights and fundamental liberties arises from the widely held belief in their validity: the question of their underlying principles cannot be avoided. But when I say that the increasingly urgent problem which we are faced with is not a question of underlying principles but guarantees, I do not mean that we think the question of underlying principles does not exist, but rather that it has, in a sense, been resolved: thus we do not have to concern ourselves any more with its solution. You could even say that today the problem of underlying principles for human rights has been resolved by the Universal Declaration of Human Rights approved by the General Assembly of the United Nations on 10 December 1948.

The Universal Declaration of Human Rights represents a unique demonstration that a value system can be considered to be founded on humanity and thus acknowledged by it: the proof is in the general consensus over its validity. Advocates of natural law would have spoken of *consensus omnium gentium* or *humani generis*.

There are three ways of demonstrating values: deduction from a constant objective fact, for example human nature; their consideration as self-evident truths; and finally the discovery that they are generally accepted within a given historical period (i.e. the test of consensus). The first method would offer us the greatest guarantee of their universal validity, if human nature really does exist, and supposing it does exist as a constant and unchanging reality, if we were capable of understanding its essence. Judging by the history of natural law, human nature can be interpreted in the most varied of fashions, and the appeal to nature has been used to justify diametrically opposed value systems. Which is the fundamental right of humankind according to its nature: the right of the strongest as Spinoza claimed or the right to liberty as Kant claimed?

The second method, the appeal to self-evidence, has the defect of putting itself beyond the requirement of proof and rejects all rational argument: in reality, as soon as we put values which are proclaimed to be self-evident to the historical test, we realize that that which was considered evident by some people at a given time was not considered evident by others in another time. It probably appeared to be evident to the authors of the Declaration of 1789 that property was 'sacre et inviolable', but today all reference to property rights as human rights has completely disappeared from the most recent documents of the United Nations.[4] Is there anyone today who does not consider it self-evident that detainees should not be tortured? Yet for many centuries torture was accepted and defended as a normal judicial procedure. When men reflected on the justification of violence, it seemed evident that 'vim vi repellere licet', while now theories of non-violence are increasingly widespread and these are based on the rejection of that principle.

The third method of justifying values is that of showing that they are supported by consensus, whereby a value has greater validity the more it is agreed to. The consensus argument replaces the test of objectivity which is considered impossible or at least extremely uncertain, with the test of inter-subjectivity. Of course this is a historical and therefore not an absolute basis, but the historical basis of consent is the only one which can be factually proved. The Universal Declaration of Human Rights can therefore be considered the greatest historical test of the 'consensus omnium gentium' in relation to a given value system. The original champions of natural law were distrustful of general consensus as the basis for natural law, and they were not completely wrong, because it was difficult to ascertain. It would have involved studying the documents produced through the obscure and troubled history of nations, as Giambattista Vico attempted to do. But now we have the document: it was approved by forty-eight states on 10 December 1948 in the General Assembly of the United Nations, and since then has been used to inspire and direct the process whereby the international community has started growing into a community not only of states but also of free and equal individuals. I do not know whether people are aware of just how much the Universal Declaration represents an unprecedented historical event, given that for the first time in history a system of fundamental principles for human behaviour has been freely and expressly accepted by the majority of the people living on this planet through their governments. Through this declaration, a system of values is *universal* (for the first time in history) not in principle, but *de facto*, in that the consensus over its validity and suitability to govern the destiny of the future community has been expressly declared (the values upheld by religions and churches, even Christianity, the most universal of the religions, has until now involved only part of humanity *de facto*, that is to say historically). Only after the Declaration, can we obtain the historical certainty that humanity in its entirety shares some common values, and finally believe in the universality of these values in a way which is historically legitimate, i.e. that by universal we mean not an objective reality, but subjectively accepted by the universe of humanity.

This universality has been achieved gradually. The development of human rights declarations can be divided into three stages. The declarations were born as philosophical theories. The first stage is to be found in philosophical works. If we do not want to go back as far as the stoic idea of the universal society of rational men (the wiseman was a citizen of the world and not of this or that fatherland), then it was the theory of natural law, whose founding father was John Locke, which developed the idea that man by virtue of being a man enjoyed certain natural rights which no one, including the state, could take away from him, and which he himself could not alienate (even if he was obliged by circumstances to alienate them, the transfer would not be valid). According to Locke, the true state of mankind is not civil society, but a state of nature in which men are free and equal. Civil society is an artificial creation which has no other purpose than to amplify natural freedom and equality. Although the theory of a state of nature has now been abandoned, the first words in the Universal Declaration of Human Rights clearly echo it: 'All men are born free and equal in dignity and rights', which is another way of saying that men are *by nature* free and equal. One could hardly avoid recalling the famous opening words to Rousseau's *The Social Contract*: 'Man *is born* free, but everywhere is in chains'. The Declaration echoes it because *de facto* people are born neither free nor equal.[5] They are free and equal in relation to an ideal birth or nature, which is indeed what the advocates of natural law were thinking of when they discussed the state of nature. The freedom and equality of human beings is not a reality, but an ideal which has to be pursued, not an existence but a value, and not a being but a must. The earliest philosophical theories of human rights are purely and simply expressions of individual thought: they are universal in that their content refers to rational man outside space and time, but they are extremely limited in effect, in that they are at best merely proposals to future legislators.

From the moment that these theories are adopted by legislators as the basis for a new concept of the state, which is no longer absolute but subject to restrictions, and no longer an end in itself but the means for achieving pre-existing ends which transcend its existence, the assertion of human rights is no longer the expression of a noble demand, but the starting point for a genuine system of rights in the strict sense of the word, i.e. positive and effective rights. This occurred with the declaration of rights proclaimed by the American States and the two French Revolutions. The second stage in the history of human rights is therefore the transition from theory to practice, from the mere perception of a right to its enactment. Through this transition, the assertion of human rights acquires concreteness but loses its universality. Rights are from then on protected as truly positive rights, but they are only valid within the state which recognizes them. However much official wordings might cling to the distinction between human rights and citizens' rights, they are no longer human rights but citizens' rights, or at least they are only human rights in as much as they are the rights of a citizen of a particular state.

The 1948 Declaration commenced the third and last stage *in which the assertion of human rights is both universal and positive*: universal in the sense that the principles it contains no longer concern only the citizens of this or that state, but all human beings, and positive in the sense that it initiates a process whose end is that human rights should no longer only be proclaimed and recognized as ideals, but effectively protected even against the state which violates them. On completion of this process, citizens' rights will have been transformed into human rights as a positive reality. In other words, they will be the rights of citizens of a political entity which has no borders, because it includes all humanity – they will be human rights in as much as they are the rights enjoyed by citizens of the world.

One might be tempted to describe the process which ended with the Universal Declaration in another way, by using the traditional categories of natural and positive law: human rights are created as universal natural rights, develop into specific positive rights, and then find their full implementation as universal positive rights. The Universal Declaration contains the embryonic synthesis of a dialectical movement which commences with the abstract universality of natural rights, passes through the concrete specificity of national positive rights, and terminates with a universality which is no longer abstract but is itself a concrete expression of universal positive rights.

When I say 'embryonic', I intend to draw attention to the fact that the Universal Declaration is only the beginning of a long process, whose final outcome we cannot yet distinguish. The Declaration is something more than a doctrinal system, but something less than a system of legal norms. As has been observed many times, the Declaration proclaims the principles which it is upholding not as legal norms, but as 'a common ideal to be achieved by all peoples and all nations'. There is a call for legal norms, but it is part of a theoretical judgement. Indeed the Preamble states that 'it is indispensable that human rights are protected by laws, *if* one wishes to avoid men being forced, as a last resort, to turn to rebellion against tyranny and oppression'. This proposition is limited to establishing a necessary link between a specific means and a specific end or, if you like, it presents a choice between two alternatives: either legal protection or rebellion. However, it does not put itself forward as the means. It indicates which is its choice, but it is not yet capable of enforcing it. It is one thing to point out which road to take, and quite another to travel all the way to the end.

When human rights were considered purely as natural rights, the only defence against their violation by the state was another natural right, the so-called right to resistance. Once constitutions recognized some of these rights as legally protected, then the natural right to resistance was transformed into the positive right to initiate legal action against state bodies. But what action can be taken by citizens of a state which has not recognized human rights as worthy of protection? Once again, the only possible course of action is represented by the right to resistance. Only the extension of this protection from a few states to all states, and the protection of these rights at a level higher than the state by the whole of the international community or part of it, can make this choice between oppression and resistance less probable. It is therefore clear that by that theoretical judgement (or that alternative, which is the same thing) the authors of the Declaration showed themselves to be perfectly aware of the means which would lead to the desired end. Again it is one thing to be aware of the means, and quite another to able to enforce it.

In stating that the Universal Declaration represented only the initial step in the final stage of the universal positivization of human rights, one is usually referring to the difficulties in implementing effective measures to guarantee them in an international community which has not yet carried out the monopolization of force that was a distinctive feature in the birth of the modern state. However, there are also problems in the very content of the Declaration. As far as the quantity and quality of the listed rights are concerned, the Declaration can make no claim to being definitive. Even human rights are historical rights which emerge gradually from the battles which human beings fight for their own emancipation and the transformation in living conditions which these struggles produce. The expression 'rights of man' is certainly emphatic, and even if that emphasis is expedient, it can be misleading because it implies that there are rights belonging to an abstract man and thus removed from the historical context, and that by contemplating this essential and eternal man we can arrive at the certain knowledge of his rights and duties. Today we know that the so-called human rights are the product of human civilization and not nature, because historical rights are changeable and therefore susceptible to transformation and growth. It is sufficient to look at the writings of the early advocates of natural law to realize how the list of rights has been getting longer and longer. Indeed Hobbes only recognized one right, the right to life. As we all know, the development of human rights has passed through three stages: the first affirmed the rights to liberty, i.e. all those rights which tend to restrict the power of the state and grants an area of freedom *from* the state to the individual or particular groups. The second stage puts forward political rights which perceive freedom not only negatively as non-interference, but positively as autonomy, and therefore have brought about a more wide-ranging and constant involvement by members of a community in the process of political power (or liberties *within* the state). The final stage has proclaimed social rights which express the development of new needs, we could even say new values, which concern wealth and equality not only on a formal level, and we could call these liberties *through* or *by means* of the state. If someone had told Locke, the champion of the rights to liberty, that all citizens should have the right to participate in politics, or even worse that they had the right to paid employment, he would have called it madness. Yet Locke had examined human nature in depth, and the human nature he observed was that of the bourgeois or merchant of the seventeenth century. It would have been impossible for him to have perceived human nature from any other point of view, to have perceived the demands and requirements of someone with another human nature or more precisely who did not have a human nature at all (given that human nature is always identified with the members of a certain class).

Thus, while the Universal Declaration of Human Rights was, as we have said, undoubtedly a starting point for the development towards the global protection of human rights, it also represented an important milestone in a process which is far from complete, a process which concerns its content (i.e. the rights it proclaimed). The rights listed in the Declaration are not the only possible human rights: they are the rights of a historical man as perceived by those who drew up the Declaration following the tragedy of the Second World War, in an epoque which commenced with the French Revolution and included the Soviet Revolution. It does not take much imagination to realize that development of technology, the transformation of social and economic conditions, widening knowledge and the intensification of the means of communication will produce such changes in the organization of human life and social relations as to engender favourable conditions for the creation of new needs and therefore new demands for freedoms and powers. Just to give a few examples, the increasing quantity and intensity of information to which a person is subjected nowadays has created an increasing need not to be deceived, upset or disturbed by obsessive and distorted propaganda; the right to truthful information is emerging in contrast to the right to freely express one's opinions. As far as participatory government is concerned, the need to participate in the exercise of economic power is being increasingly felt as an extension of the right to participate in the political process which is now recognized everywhere but not always applied, because economic power is becoming more and more a determining factor in political decisions, and decisive in the choices which affect everybody's life. Finally, the field of social rights is undergoing continuous change: just as the demands for social protection were created by the industrial revolution, rapid economic and technological development will probably lead to new demands which at the moment we could not even predict. The Universal Declaration represents the historical awareness that humanity has its own fundamental values in the second half of the twentieth century. It is a synthesis of the past and an inspiration for the future, but it is not a tablet carved in stone once and for ever.

By this I mean that today the international community is not only confronted with the problem of preparing valid guarantees for those rights, but also the question of continually improving the content of the Declaration by articulating it, clarifying its detail and updating it so that it does not turn into rigid and ossified formulae, which become emptier as they become more mystified. This problem has been confronted by international bodies over recent years through a series of acts which demonstrate just how much these bodies are aware of the historical nature of the original document, and the need to keep it alive by making it grow from within. It is a genuine development or perhaps more of a gradual evolution of the Declaration which has generated and continues to generate further documents interpreting or integrating the initial document.

I shall restrict myself to a few examples: the Declaration of the Rights of Children adopted by the General Assembly on 20 November 1959 refers in its Preamble to the Universal Declaration, and immediately after this reference presents the question of childrens' rights as a specification of the solution found for human rights. When it states that children require '*special* protection and *particular* care, because of their physical and intellectual immaturity', it is clear that the rights of children are being considered as a *ius singulare* in relation to a *ius commune*: the importance attributed to them in the new document derives from the specification of the generality, which adheres to the maxim *suum cuique tribuere*. Consider Article 2 of the Universal Declaration which condemns any discrimination based on sex and race, as well as on religion, language, etc. As far as the discrimination based on sex is concerned, the Declaration cannot go further than this general statement, because it must be understood that where 'individuals' are discussed in the text, it is referring to men and women without distinction. But since 20 December 1952, the General Assembly has approved a Convention on the Political Rights of Women, which in the first three articles provides for non-discrimination in relation to electoral suffrage, candidature and the possibility of entering all public office. As far as racial discrimination is concerned, suffice it to recall that on 20 November 1963 the General Assembly approved a declaration (followed two years later by a convention) on the elimination of all forms of racial discrimination, which in eleven articles specified some typical cases of discriminatory action, and considered specific and well-defined discriminatory practices, such as segregation and in particular apartheid (Art. 5): specific practices which clearly could not be provided for in a general declaration.

Perhaps one of the most interesting and conspicuous examples of growth in human rights is the question of decolonization, which it should be remembered occurred in its most decisive historical forms after the Declaration. Well, in the Declaration on the Granting of Independence to Colonial Countries and Peoples (approved on 14 December 1960) there is the usual general reference to human rights considered as a whole, but there is something more: the assertion from the very first article that 'the subjection of peoples to a foreign domination is a negation of fundamental human rights'. This constituted a complete addendum to the text of the Universal Declaration, and it is not difficult to imagine the explosive effect. Indeed it is one thing to state as the Universal Declaration does in Article 2, 2 that 'no distinction shall be made on the basis of the political, legal or international status of the country or territory to which a person belongs', and quite another to consider 'the subjection of peoples to foreign domination' to be contrary to human rights, as does the Declaration of Independence. The first statement concerns the individual, and the second an entire people. One stops at the non-discrimination of the individual, and the other extends to collective autonomy. This, in fact, relates back to the principle that every people has a right to self-determination, which was proclaimed at the time of the French Revolution and became one of the inspirations for the nationalist movements over the last two centuries. It is precisely this principle which reappears in Article 2 of the Declaration of

Independence. It is clear, therefore, that there is a need to affirm the fundamental rights of peoples which were not necessarily included amongst the right of the individual which the Universal Declaration exclusively referred to, and that this need has evolved alongside individual rights because of decolonization and the awakening conscience of new values that this process has expressed. In the latest and most important documents concerning human rights which have been approved by the United Nations, we have reached the stage of accepting the principle of self-determination as a primary principle or principle of principles. The Treaty on Economic, Social and Cultural Rights and the Treaty on Civil and Political Rights, which were both approved by the General Assembly of the United Nations on 16 December 1966, commence with the statement: 'All peoples have the right to self-determination', and continue: 'By virtue of this right, they freely decide their political constitution, and freely pursue their economic, social and cultural development'. Article 3 emphasizes that 'states . . . must promote the implementation of the right of peoples to self-determination.'

I am not intending to list all the activities of United Nations bodies for the promotion of human rights, which have constituted a development and clarification of the Universal Declaration, and I am mainly thinking here of the agreements on labour questions and trade union freedom which have been adopted by the International Labour Organization. Yet I could hardly fail to refer to the Convention for the Prevention and Suppression of Genocide approved by the General Assembly on 9 December 1958, which extended Articles 3 and 5 of the Universal Declaration which concern an individual's right to life, personal safety, and not to be enslaved or treated in a cruel, inhuman or degrading manner, to groups of human beings considered as a whole. Yet again, new rights for groups of persons, peoples and nations are emerging from the rights of man as an individual. An interesting if somewhat disturbing case which arises from this Magna Charta championing the peoples is Article 47 of the Treaty on Civil and Political Rights, which speaks of 'an inherent right of all peoples to enjoy and dispose of their riches and natural resources fully and freely'. The reasons for such a statement are not difficult to understand, but what the consequences would be if it was applied strictly to the letter, would be rather difficult to predict.

I said at the beginning that what matters is the protection of human rights rather their creation. I need hardly add that it is not sufficient to proclaim them in order to protect them. Up till now I have only talked about statements of varying degrees of articulateness, but the real problem we are faced with is the question of what measures have and can be invented to protect them effectively. We can only observe that we are on an impassable road, and the travellers walking along this road either can see clearly but have their legs tied, or their legs are free but, alas, they are blindfolded. First of all, one should distinguish between two types of difficulty: one which is strictly speaking legal and political; and a second which is substantial, i.e. inherent in the content of the rights concerned.

The first difficulty depends on the nature of the international community itself, or more precisely the type of interrelationships between individual states and between each individual state and the international community taken as a whole. One could apply a former distinction used in a previous age to describe relations between the church and state, and claim that international bodies possess a *vis directiva* and not *coactiva* in relation to their member states, although this is the kind of approximation which is unavoidable with such clear-cut distinctions. When we talk about legal protection and we wish to distinguish it from other forms of social control, we are thinking about the protection the citizen has, if he or she has it, within the state, which is therefore protection based on *vis coactiva*. The effectiveness of *vis directiva* and the difference between *vis directiva* and *vis coactiva* in terms of effectiveness, is a complex problem which cannot be dealt with here. I shall limit myself to the following observation: if *vis directiva* is to achieve its purpose, then one or other of the following two conditions must apply, or better still both together:

1 Those who exercise the *vis directiva* must be extremely authoritative, i.e. if they do not inspire a mixture of reverence and fear, they must at least inspire respect.
2 Those to whom it is directed must be extremely reasonable, i.e. they must have a general disposition to consider arguments based on reason and not just on force.

However unsuitable all generalizations and however varied the relationships between states and international bodies, it has to be admitted that there are cases in which one or other of these conditions is lacking, and some in which both are lacking. And it is precisely in these cases that it is more likely that there will be insufficient or even no protection for those human rights which the international body is supposed to safeguard. Contempt for human rights within a country and a lack of respect for the international bodies outside go together. The more a government is authoritarian towards the freedoms of its citizens, the more it is libertarian (allow me to use the term) in relation to international authority.

Modern political theory follows on from the old differentiation but with greater precision. It distinguishes substantially two forms of social control, *influence* and *power*. By 'influence' it means the method of control which determines another's actions by bringing pressure to bear upon the decision-making process. By 'power' it means the method of control which determines another's behaviour by making all other actions impossible. Even on the basis of this distinction, it is clear that there is a difference between legal protection in the strict sense of the term and international guarantees: the former uses that form of social control which is defined as 'power', and the latter are founded purely on influence. Let us consider Felix Oppenheim's theory which distinguishes between three forms of influence, persuasion/dissuasion, deterrence and conditioning, and three forms of power (or restraint), physical violence, legal restraint and the threat of severe deprivations.[6] Control by international bodies corresponds fairly well to the three forms of influence, but falls short of the first form of power. It is precisely the first form of power which constitutes the basis for the kind of protection which by long tradition we have become accustomed to defining as legal. Far be it from me to involve myself in time-wasting quibbles over words: substantially it is a question of finding out what possible forms of social control exist, and on this basis establishing which are currently being applied or could be applied by the international community. This would then involve distinguishing between the more effective and less effective methods of impeding deviant behaviour or reducing it to a minimum, and asking ourselves how effective are the measures which are currently applied or could be applied at international level to safeguarding human rights.

The activities which have been carried out so far by international bodies in order to safeguard human rights could be considered under three categories: *promotion, monitoring* and *guarantees*.[7] 'Promotion' means the series of actions directed towards a twin objective:

1 to induce those states which have no specific system of regulations to safeguard human rights to introduce one;
2 to induce those states which do have one, to improve it both in terms of the substance of the law (number and quality of rights to be safeguarded) and the procedures (number and quality of the legal controls).

'Monitoring activity' signifies the series of measures which various international bodies put into effect in order to monitor the degree to which their recommendations have been met and conventions adhered to. Two typical monitoring methods, which for instance were both adopted by the 1966 treaties mentioned above, are *reports* which each state, as signatory to the agreement, undertakes to submit on the measures taken to safeguard human rights in relation to the treaty concerned (see Art. 40), and *communiqués* by which a state, as party to the agreement, denounces another, as party to the agreement, for the non-fulfilment of the obligations arising from the treaty (see Art. 41).[8] Finally by 'guarantee activity' (perhaps it would be better just to say 'guarantees' in the strict sense of the word) it is meant the organization of fully-fledged legal safeguards at international level which substitute the national ones. The distinction between the first two forms of safeguard for human rights and the third is extremely clear-cut. While 'promotion' and 'monitoring' are both exclusively concerned with existing guarantees or their establishment within a state – i.e. they tend to reinforce and improve on the national legal system – the third form aims at the creation of a new and higher jurisdiction and the replacement of national guarantees by international ones, should the former prove to be insufficient or even completely lacking.

As is well known, the European Convention on Human Rights which was signed in Rome on 4 November 1950 and came into effect on 3 September 1953, provided for the latter type of guarantee by a procedure of individual applications to the European Commission on Human Rights that was heralded as highly innovative (see Art. 25).[9] It is an innovation which at the moment represents the most advanced point in the current system of international protection for human rights. Thus one will only be able to talk of international safeguards for human rights when an international jurisdiction will be able to superimpose itself on the national jurisdictions, and the safeguards *within* the state, which are the main feature of the current phase, are transformed into safeguards *against* the state.

It should be remembered that the struggle for human rights within individual states was accompanied by establishment of representative regimes, i.e. the dissolution of the states with a concentrated power base. Although all historical analogies should be treated with great caution, the struggle for the affirmation of rights including those against the state probably presupposes a change in the concept of power outside the state in relation to other states and an increase in the representative nature of international bodies, and this change is already under way, albeit very slowly. The example of the European Convention shows that forms of international guarantee are today more advanced where the national guarantees are also more advanced and, strictly speaking, where there is least need. We say that 'constitutional guarantees' exist in those states where there is a properly functioning system of guarantees for human rights. In the world there are states with and without properly functioning 'constitutional guarantees'. There can be no doubt that it is the citizens in the states without properly functioning constitutional guarantees who most need international protection. Yet these states are the very ones which are least inclined to accept the changes to the international community that would open the way to the establishment of a well-functioning legal system to protect human rights fully. To put it in graphic terms, we are now in a situation in which the international safeguarding of human rights is more possible where it is not perhaps completely necessary, and less possible where it is most needed.

Apart from the legal and political difficulties, the safeguard of human rights faces difficulties which are inherent in the very nature of these rights. It is surprising how little concern there is over these difficulties in general. As the majority of the rights have by now become part of a common moral attitude, it is felt that their application is equally straightforward. Instead, it is terribly complicated. On the one hand, the general consensus about them leads us to believe that they have an absolute value, and on the other, the single generic term 'human rights' suggests a uniform category. Yet for the most part human rights are not absolute, and they do not constitute a uniform category.

By 'absolute value' I mean the status which belongs to very few human rights, whereby they are valid in all situations and for all human beings without distinction. This privileged status depends on a situation which rarely occurs: it is a situation in which fundamental rights do not compete with other fundamental rights. One has to start from the obvious statement that you cannot introduce a right in favour of one category of persons without suppressing a right of other categories of persons. The right not to be subjected to slavery implies the elimination of the right to own slaves, just as the right not to be tortured implies the suppression of the right to torture. However, these two can be considered absolute, because the action which is considered illegitimate through the institution and protection of these rights is universally condemned. Proof of this can be found in the European Convention on Human Rights which explicitly excludes these rights from the suspension in the protection of other rights in the event of war or danger to the public (see Art. 15, § 2). Yet in the majority of cases concerning human rights two equally fundamental human rights conflict with each other, and it is impossible to protect one unconditionally without making the other inoperative. Take, for example, the right to freedom of expression on the one hand, and the right not to be deceived, provoked, scandalized, offended, libelled, or vilified on the other. In these cases, which are the majority, one has to refer to fundamental rights which are not absolute but relative, in the sense that at a certain stage their protection encounters an insuperable obstacle in the protection of another right which is also fundamental and in competition. Given that the cut-off point where one right ends and the other commences is difficult to establish and is always a matter of opinion, the demarcation in the context of fundamental human rights is extremely variable and cannot be established once and for all.

Some articles of the European Convention of Human Rights are, as is well known, divided into two paragraphs, the first of which establishes a right, and the second lists exceptions which on occasions can be numerous. There are situations in which a right which some groups consider fundamental cannot even gain recognition, because the opposing fundamental right continues to prevail, as in the case of conscientious objection. Which is more fundamental: the right not to kill or the right of the community as a whole to defend itself against outside aggression? My conscience, the value system of the group I belong to, or humanity's moral conscience in a given moment in history? We can hardly fail to realize that each of these criteria is extremely vague, too vague for the implementation of the principle of certainty which a judicial system appears to require in order to apportion right and wrong impartially.

When I say that all human rights constitute a heterogeneous category, I refer to the fact that as soon human rights include social rights as well as liberties, then the category as a whole includes rights which are incompatible with each other, i.e. rights which cannot be protected without restricting or suppressing the protection of others. One can fantasize as much as one wants about a society which is both free and just, and in which all liberties and social rights are universally implemented at the same time, but the real societies that we are confronted with are free in as much as they lack justice, and they are just in as much as they lack freedom. Let me clarify that by 'liberties' I mean rights which guarantee when the state cannot intervene, and 'powers' as rights which require the intervention of the state for their implementation. Well, liberties and powers are incompatible, and not, as some believe, complementary. To give a banal example, the increased power to purchase a motor car has diminished the freedom to travel by road almost to point of paralysis. A slightly less banal example is the extension of the social right to go to school to the age of fourteen which in Italy has suppressed the freedom to choose one type of school rather than another. But perhaps there is no need for examples: the contemporary society in which we live, which features an ever-increasing organizational efficiency, is a society in which every day we acquire a piece of power in exchange for a slice of freedom. This distinction between two types of human rights, whose total and simultaneous implementation is impossible, is also dictated by the fact that at a theoretical level there are two opposing and contrasting concepts of human rights: one liberal and one socialist.

The difference between the two concepts consists precisely in the conviction that a choice must be made between the two types of rights, or at least a priority must be established and thus a different criterion based on the choice or priority made. Even though both of them claim to synthesize both types of rights, history has put the regimes that represent them to a severe test. All we can expect from the development of the two types of regime is not a synthesis but a compromise (a kind of synthesis perhaps, but a provisional one). But here again we are faced with the problem of which basic criteria can be used for evaluating the compromise. No one is able to give a reply which could lift humanity above the danger of falling into tragic errors. The fundamental values of human civilization up to the present moment have emerged from the proclamation of human rights, but the final values are antinomical and this is the problem.

One last consideration. I have spoken of the difficulties which arise from within the category of human rights itself, if taken in its entirety. I still have to refer to a difficulty which concerns the conditions of their implementation. Not everything which is desirable and worth striving for is achievable. In order to implement human rights objective conditions are required which often do not depend on the good intentions of those who proclaim them or the sympathies of those who have the means to protect them. Even the most liberal of states is obliged to suspend some liberties during time of war, just as the most socialist of states is unable to guarantee the right to equal distribution of wealth during times of famine. It is well known that the terrible problem which faces developing countries today is that they find themselves in an economic situation which does not allow the protection of the majority of social rights, whatever their ideals. The right to work was born with the industrial revolution, and is closely linked to its realization. It is not sufficient to establish or proclaim such a right. It is not even enough to protect it. The question of its implementation is neither philosophical nor moral. Nor is it judicial. It is a problem whose solution depends on a certain development of society, and as such it challenges the most progressive constitution and undermines the most perfect mechanism of legal guarantees.

I believe that every discussion on human rights must take into account all the substantial and procedural difficulties which I have briefly referred to, if it is to avoid the risk of becoming an academic exercise. The implementation of a better system for protecting human rights is linked to the global development of human civilization. If the problem is taken in isolation, there is a risk not only that it will not be resolved, but that its true significance will not even be understand. It will elude anyone who looks at it in isolation. One cannot abstract the problem of human rights from the great problems of our time, which are war and poverty, the absurd contrast between the excess of *power* which created the conditions for a genocidal war and the excess of *impotence* which has condemned the great majority of humanity to hunger. This is the only context in which we can approach the problem of human rights realistically. We must not be so pessimistic that we give up in despair, but neither must we be so optimistic that we become over-confident.

I would advise anyone who wishes to carry out an unbiased examination of the development of human rights after the Second World War to carry out this sobering exercise: to read the Universal Declaration and look around. Such a person would be obliged to recognize that in spite of the enlightened advances of philosophers, the bold formulations of lawyers and the efforts of well-intentioned politicians, there is still a long way to go. Human history, in spite of its millennia, will appear to have just commenced given the enormity of the tasks ahead.

Notes

1   See previous essay which first appeared under the title 'L'Illusion du fondement absolu', in *Les Fondements des droits de l'homme* (Florence: n. pub., 1966), p. 8 (and also p. 170), and then in Italian as 'Sul fondamento

dei diritti dell'uomo', *Rivista internazionale di filosofia del diritto*, vol. XLII (1965), pp. 302–9.

2 This was the introductory paper read at the National Conference on Human Rights, held in Turin from 1 to 3 December 1967, and organized by the Società Italiana per l'Organizzazione Internazionale.

3 I am quoting from *La comunità internazionale*, vol. XXII (1967), p. 337. For this and other information I referred to the article by F. Capotorti, 'Le Nazioni Unite per il progresso dei diritti dell'uomo. Risultati e prospettive', *La communità internazionale*, vol. XXII (1967), pp. 11–35.

4 I refer here to the *International Pact on Economic, Social and Cultural Rights*, which together with the *International Pact on Civil Rights* was approved by the General Assembly of the United Nations on 16 December 1966.

5 I have discussed this point elsewhere: 'Eguaglianza e dignità degli uomini', in *Diritti dell'uomo e Nazioni Unite* (Padua: Cedam, 1963), pp. 29–42.

6 F. Oppenheim, *Dimensions of Freedom* (New York: St Martin's Press, 1961), pp. 25–36.

7 This classification should be taken with a grain of salt. It is not always easy to distinguish where promotion ends and control commences, and where control ends and guarantee commences. It is a *continuum* in which three moments can be distinguished for didactic ease. For a more in-depth study of the problem, I refer to two works by A. Cassese: 'Il controllo internazionale sul rispetto della libertà sindacale nel quadro delle attuali tendenze in materia di protezione internazionale dei diritti dell'uomo', in *Comunicazioni e studi* (published by the Istituto di Diritto Internazionale e Straniero dell'Università di Milano), 1966, pp. 293–418, and 'Il sistema di garanzia della Convenzione dell' ONU sull'eliminazione di ogni forma di discriminazione razziale', *Rivista di diritto internazionale*, vol. L (1967), pp. 270–336 and bibliography.

8 These problems are dealt with in greater depth by Capotorti's article referred to in §§ 5 and 6. The author draws attention to art. 22 of the ILO charter and art. VIII of the UNESCO charter.

9 See G. Sperduti's preface to *The European Convention on Human Rights* (Strasbourg: European Council, 1962).

3 The Age of Rights

In a recent interview, I was asked whether I could see any positive signs among so many causes for concern, following a lengthy discussion about the most worrying features of our time as far as the future of humanity is concerned: the three we discussed most of all were the accelerating and as yet uncontrolled increase in population, the accelerating and as yet uncontrolled degeneration of the environment, and the accelerating, uncontrolled and nonsensical increase in the destructive power of armaments. I replied that, yes, I could see at least one: the increasing importance given to the recognition of human rights in international debates, among cultured people and politicians, in working groups and government conferences.

Clearly the problem is not a new one. At least since the beginning of the modern era, through the spread of doctrines based on natural law at first, and then in the declarations of human rights included in the constitutions of liberal states, the problem has followed the birth, development and affirmation of the constitutional state around the world. However, it is also true that it was not until after the Second World War that this question changed from being a national one to being an international one, and involved all peoples for the first time in history.

The Introduction to the anthology of documents edited by Gregorio Peces-Barba, *Derecho positivo de los derechos humanos*, presents and comments upon the three evolutionary processes of positivization, generalization and internationalization in the history of human rights, which have emerged with increasing force.[1]

1. There are various approaches to the subject of human rights. They can be philosophical, historical, ethical, legal or political. Each approach is linked to all the others, but can also be considered independently. For today's discussion, I have chosen yet another approach, which I know is risky and perhaps a little pretentious in that it should embrace and transcend all the others: the only name that I could give it is the *philosophy of history*.

I know very well that the philosophy of history is discredited today, especially in Italy after Benedetto Croce decreed its demise. Philosophy of history is now considered a typically nineteenth-century discipline whose time has passed. Perhaps the last great attempt at philosophy of history was Karl Jaspers's work, *Vom Ursprung und Ziel der Geschichte* (1949),[2] which in spite of its fascinating representation of the great epochs of human history, was soon forgotten and has not given rise to any serious debate. However, when faced with a broad subject like human rights, it is difficult to resist the temptation to go beyond purely narrative history.

Whether or not they accept its relevance, historians generally believe that philosophy of history when faced with an event or series of events, poses the question of its 'sense' according to a finalistic (or teleological) concept of history (and this is valid for natural history as well as human history) which considers the course of history overall from its origin to its fulfilment of an end or a *telos*. For anyone who takes this point of view, events cease to be facts requiring description, narration, situation in time, and perhaps explanation according to research methods and techniques developed and widely used by historians, and they become *signs* or *clues* which reveal a process moving in a pre-established direction, which does not have to be intentional. In spite of the historian's diffidence or even aversion to philosophy of history, it is arguable that we can totally exclude the possibility that the historical narration of great events hides a finalistic perspective, even if the historian is not fully aware of it.

It is doubtful that a historian of the *ancien régime* can avoid being influenced in his or her narration of the events by their final outcome in the Great Revolution. It is difficult to avoid the temptation to interpret them as forewarnings of a pre-established end which is in implicit in them.

Man is a teleological animal, who generally acts with a view to an end projected into the future. One can only make 'sense' of a given action, by considering its end. Philosophy of history's approach represents the transposition of this finalistic interpretation from the action of the single individual to humanity in its totality, as though humanity were an individual on a grand scale to whom we can attribute the characteristics of an individual on a small scale. What makes philosophy of history problematic is precisely this transposition which lacks any convincing proof. The important thing for whoever wishes to carry out this transposition, whether or not it is legitimate for the professional historian, is to be aware that he or she is moving on to a terrain which, to use Kant's words, we could call prophetic history – that is to say, a history whose purpose is not cognitive, but admonitive, exhortative or just suggestive.

2. In one of his last writings Kant asked himself whether 'the human race is continually improving'. He felt that he could give an affirmative answer to this question, which he thought belonged to a prophetic concept of history, albeit with some hesitation.

In attempting to identify an event which could be considered a 'sign' of man's disposition to progress, he pointed to the enthusiasm which had been engendered in world public opinion by the French Revolution, which could only have been caused by 'humanity's moral disposition'. He commented that 'true enthusiasm always refers to that which is ideal, to that which is purely moral . . . and cannot graft itself onto individual interests'. The cause of this enthusiasm, and therefore its prophetic sign (*signum prognosticum*) of humanity's moral disposition was, according to Kant, the appearance on the historical scene of 'a people's right not to be obstructed by other forces from giving itself a civil constitution which it considers to be good'. By 'civil constitution' Kant intended a constitution in harmony with men's natural rights, so that 'those who obey the law must also act as a unified body of legislators.'[3]

By defining the right of every man to obey only those laws in whose legislation he has himself participated as a natural right,

Kant defined liberty as autonomy, as the power to legislate over oneself. Besides, at the beginning of *Grounding for the Metaphysics of Morals*, which was written in the same period, he solemnly and categorically stated, as though it were a matter beyond discussion, that once law was understood as the moral faculty to govern the behaviour of others, man had innate and acquired rights, and liberty was the only innate right in the sense of being transmitted to man from nature and not from an established authority. In othe words, liberty was independence from any constriction imposed by another will: liberty as autonomy.

My theory, which is inspired by this extraordinary passage of Kant's, is that from the point of view of the philosophy of history, the current increasingly widespread and intense debate on human rights can be interpreted as a 'prophetic sign' (*signum prognosticum*) of humanity's moral progress, given that it is so widespread as to involve all the peoples of the world and so intense as to be on the agenda of the most authoritative international judicial bodies.

I do not consider myself an advocate of blind faith in progress. The idea of progress has been central to philosophy of history in past centuries, following the demise of the idea of cycles which was prevalent in the classical and pre-Christian era, and the idea of regression, though the demise of this last idea which Kant defined as terroristic may not be definitive. By saying 'not definitive', I am myself suggesting the idea that the continuous rebirth of past ideas once considered dead for ever, which is an argument against the idea of indeterminate and irreversible progress. While not being a dogmatic supporter of irresistable progress, I am also not a dogmatic supporter of the opposite argument. The only assertion I feel I can make with a certain confidence is that human history is ambiguous, and responds differently according to who is asking the questions and from what point of view. In spite of this, we cannot avoid questioning ourselves about man's destiny, just as we cannot avoid questioning ourselves about his origin. I repeat again that we can only do this by examining the signs left by events, as Kant did when he asked himself if the human race was continually improving.

Let it be quite clear that scientific and technical progress is one thing, and moral progress is quite another. It is not a question of taking up the perennial controversy over the relationship between the two. I shall limit myself to stating that, while there seems no doubt that scientific and technical progress is a reality, as up till now it has demonstrated the twin characteristics of continuity and irreversibility, it is much more difficult, and perhaps even risky, to deal with the question of whether moral progress is a reality. There are at least two reasons for this. First, the concept of morality is itself problematic. And second even if we were all in agreement on how to interpret morality, no one has yet discovered a yardstick by which to measure the moral progress of a nation, or indeed of all humanity, while on the other hand scientific and technical progress clearly can be measured in this way.

3. The concept of morality is problematic. I certainly do not intend to put forward a solution. I can simply say what in my opinion is the best way to approach the problem, and what is the most useful way to make people understand the problem, even in terms of didactic efficiency, and to give meaning to the extremely obscure concept which is generally referred to as 'moral conscience' (except in terms of a religious perception of the world, but here I am attempting to give a rational-ethical response). Kant, it is true, said the two things which filled him with wonder were moral conscience and the star-filled sky. But wonder is no explanation, and can in fact derive from an illusion and generate others in turn. Because of the immense, not to say exclusive, influence of Christian education in the formation of Europeans, what we call 'moral conscience' is linked to the formation and growth of awareness of the state of suffering, poverty, destitution and general unhappiness in which humankind finds itself in the world, and the feeling that such a state is unbearable.

As I have said, human history is ambiguous for anyone who wants to make 'sense' of it. It contains a mixture, a confusion of good and evil. But who would ever dare to deny that evil has always prevailed over good, as has pain over joy, unhappiness over happiness, and death over life? I know very well that the statement of a reality does not explain or justify it. For my part, I can say without hesitation that theological explanations and justifications do not convince me, and the rational ones are partial and often contradictory, so that you cannot accept one without rejecting the other (but the reasons for making a choice are weak, while each is supported by strong arguments). In spite of my inability to offer a convincing explanation or justification, I feel reasonably confident about asserting that the dark area of human history is much greater than the light area (and this is even truer of natural history).

Yet I would not deny that the enlightened side does occasionally appear, albeit for a brief period. Even today when the entire course of human history seems threatened with death, there are areas of light which even the most convinced pessimist could not ignore: the abolition of slavery, and the suppression of the death penalty and the tortures which in many countries accompanied it. I would place the growing interest of movements, parties and governments in the affirmation, recognition and protection of human rights in the forefront of the enlightened area, together with the ecological and pacifist movements.

This striving towards good, or at least towards the correction, containment and destruction of evil, which is an essential feature of the human world compared with the animal world, arises from the previously mentioned awareness of the suffering and unhappiness in which humanity lives and the need to escape from them. Man has always attempted to overcome his awareness of death which creates anguish, either by the integration of the single individual in the group to which he belongs which is considered immortal, or the religious belief in immortality and reincarnation. Man's efforts to transform the world which surrounds him and to make it less hostile rely just as much upon rules of behaviour which modify relations between individuals in order to make peaceful co-existence possible and allow groups to survive as they do upon techniques for producing instruments. Tools and behavioural rules form the world of 'culture' as opposed to the world of 'nature'.

According to Hobbes's theory of *homo homini lupus*, man reacted to finding himself in a world which was hostile, both in terms of nature and other men, by inventing survival techniques in relation to the former and defensive techniques in relation to the latter. The defensive techniques consist of systems of rules which reduce aggressive impulses by punishments, and encourage collaborative impulses and solidarity by rewards.

At the beginning, rules are essentially imperative, either negative or positive, and they aim to establish desirable behaviour or to avoid undesirable behaviour by recourse to sanctions in this world or the next. The Ten Commandments immediately come to mind, and are just the most familiar example. For centuries they have been and still are the essential moral code of the Christian world, to the extent that they have been identified with the law inscribed on men's hearts or in conformity with nature. But one could cite innumerable other examples from the Code of Hammurabi to the Laws of the Twelve Tables. The moral world, as we have understood it here, is born with the formulation, imposition and application of commands and prohibitions. Great legislators such as Minos, Lycurgus and Solon, were heroes of the classical world, and admiration for legislators continued until Rousseau, who stated: 'He who dares to undertake the making of a people's institutions ought to feel himself capable, so to speak, of changing human nature.'[4] Great moral works were treatises on the law: from Plato's *The Laws* and Cicero's *On Laws* to Montesquieu's *The Spirit of the Laws*. Plato's work commences with an Athenian asking 'Tell me, gentlemen, to whom do you give credit for your codes of law? Is it a God or a man?' and Cleinias replies: 'A god, sir, a god.'[5] The characteristics which Cicero attributes to natural law are *vetare et jubere*: to prohibit and command. Although Montesquieu believed that man was made to live in society, he can forget about the existence of others, so 'legislators have returned him to his duties by political and civil laws'.[6] It can be seen from these quotations, which could be backed up by infinite others, that the primary function of the law is to constrict and not to liberate, to limit and not to open up areas of liberty, to straighten the twisted tree and not to allow it to grow wild.

Using a common metaphor, one could say that rights and duties represent two sides of the same coin. But which side is which? It depends on how you look at the coin. Well, the moral coin has traditionally been considered more from the side representing duties than the one for rights.

It is not difficult to understand the reason. The moral question was originally considered more from society's point of view than that of the individual. Nor could it have been otherwise: the function attributed to the rules of conduct was to protect the group as a whole rather than the single individual. Originally the function of the precept 'thou shalt not kill' was not to protect the single member of the group so much as to remove one of the fundamental reasons for a group's disintegration. The best proof of this is that this precept, which is justifiably considered a moral cornerstone, was valid for members of the same group, but not of other groups.

To continue the metaphor, which is I think sufficiently clear, the coin had to be reversed in order to bring about the change-over from a legal code based on duties to one based on rights, and for the moral question to be considered from the individual's point of view as well, and no longer from that of society alone. What was required was a genuine Copernican revolution, a revolution in its outcome if not in the manner it occurred. It is not necessarily the case that a radical revolution must be revolutionary in style. It can occur gradually. Here I am talking of revolution in the Kantian sense, as an inversion in the point of observance.

I have used another distinction to explain the nature of this turning-point, even though it is limited to the political sphere (politics are an aspect of morality in general): the quintessential political relationship is the relationship between rulers and the ruled, between those who have the power to enforce their decisions on members of a group, and those who are subject to those decisions. Now this relationship can be considered from the point of view of the rulers or the ruled, and for centuries the former viewpoint of the rulers prevailed. The object of politics has always been government, good government or bad government. In other words, it is about how power is achieved, how it is exercised, what duties are allocated to magistrates, and what powers to the government, how they are distinguished and how they inter-relate, how laws are introduced and enforced, how wars are declared and peace settled, and how ministers and ambassadors are appointed. Think of the great metaphors which have been used over the centuries to illustrate what the art of politics is really about: the shepherd, the helmsman, the charioteer, the weaver or the doctor. They all refer to activities which typify a position of control: the guidance which a ruler must exert in order to lead the individuals in his trust towards the common objective requires the means of command, or the organization of a fragmented universe requires a firm hand in order to be solid and stable. The

guardianship must occasionally be robust in order to deal effi-
ciently with a sick body.

The single individual is essentially an object of power or, at the
very most, a passive subject. Political treatises speak mainly of his
duties rather than his rights, and his principal duty is to obey the
laws. The power of command has, at the other end of the relationship, the corresponding theme of political obligation, which is
precisely the obligation to obey the law, considered of primary
importance for the citizen. If there is an active subject which can
be discerned in this relationship, it is not the single individual
with his original rights to be asserted against the power of government, but rather the people as a whole, in which the individual
disappears as a holder of rights.

4. The great turning-point started in the West with the Christian
concept of life, according to which all men were brothers in as
much as they were children of God. Yet in reality brotherhood
does not in itself have any moral value. Both the Scriptures
and the secular history of Italy started with a fratricide. The philosophical doctrine which made the individual and not society
the starting point for the construction of a doctrine of morality
and rights was the doctrine of natural law, which can in many
ways be considered a secularization of Christian ethics, and
this was certainly the intention of its founders ('*etsi daremus
non esse deum*'). While for Lucretius, men in the state of nature
lived 'in the manner of beasts' ('*more ferarum*'), for Cicero they
wandered in the fields like beasts ('*in agris bestiarum modo vagaban-
tur*'), and for Hobbes men also behaved like wolves in the state
of nature. Locke, who was the main inspiration for legislators
on human rights, commenced his chapter on the state of nature
with these words: 'To understand political power aright,
and derive it from its original, we must consider what state all
men are naturally in, and that it is a state of perfect freedom to
order their actions and dispose of their possessions and persons
as they think fit, within the bounds of the law of nature, without
asking leave, or depending upon the will of any other man.'[7]
Initially then, according to Locke, there was no suffering, misery
and condemnation to an 'animal state', as Vico defined it, but
there was a state of freedom, albeit within the limitations of the
laws.

It is precisely from Locke onwards that it can be seen that the doctrine of natural rights presupposes an individualistic concept of society and therefore of the state, in continual opposition to the much more solid and ancient concept of society as an organic whole more important than the constituent parts.

The individualistic concept had difficulty in making headway, because it is generally considered an instigator of disunity, discord and the break-up of established order. It is striking how Hobbes contrasts individualistic origins (there are only individuals in the state of nature, and no ties between them – each is closed into his own sphere of interests which conflict with the interests of others) with the persistent representation of the state as a magnified body, an 'artificial man', whose soul is the sovereign, whose joints are the magistrates, whose nerves are punishments and rewards, etc. The organic concept is so persistent that even on the eve of the French Revolution which proclaimed the rights of the individual in relation to the state, Edmund Burke wrote: 'Individuals pass like shadows; the commonwealth is fixed and stable'.[8] After the Revolution in the period of the Restoration, Lamennais accused individualism of destroying 'the very idea of obedience and duty, thereby destroying both power and law'. Then he asks: 'what then remains but a terrifying confusion of interests, passions and diverse opinions?'[9]

According to the individualistic concept, the individual comes first, and then comes the state, not vice versa; it should be stressed that this means the single individual has intrinsic value. The state is made for the individual and not the individual for the state, or to quote the famous Article 2 of the 1789 Declaration, the preservation of the natural and indefeasible rights of man is 'the purpose of every political association'. This inversion of the traditional relationship between individual and state also involves the inversion of the traditional relationship between rights and duties. In relation to individuals, rights now come before duties, and in relation to the state, duties come first and then rights. The same inversion occurs in relation to the purpose of the state which for the organic argument was the Ciceronian concept of concord (which the Greeks termed *omonoia*), or the struggle against the factions which lacerate and murder the body politic, while for individualism it is the growth of the individual free as far as is possible from external conditioning. Equally in relation to justice, the most appropriate definition for an organic concept is the Platonic one which perceived each part of the social body as being obliged to carry out its own function, while for the individualistic concept, it is right that all persons should be treated in such a manner that they are able to achieve their own goals, especially happiness which is the quintessential individual goal.

Today the social sciences are dominated by a trend called *'methodological* individualism', according to which the study of society must commence from the study of the behaviour of individuals. This is not the place to discuss the limitations of this trend, but there are at least two other forms of individualism without which the human rights point of view would become incomprehensible: *ontological* individualism which starts from the premise that each individual is autonomous in relation to all the others and is of equal dignity (it is difficult to say whether this premise is more metaphysical or theological; and *ethical* individualism according to which each individual is a moral agent. All three versions of individualism combine to give a positive connotation to a term which had negative connotations for both revolutionary and conservative or reactionary currents of thought. Individualism is the philosophical basis for democracy: one person, one vote. As such it has and will always oppose holistic concepts of society and history, wherever they originate, as these share a contempt for democracy perceived as a form of government in which everyone is free and empowered to take decisions of concern to themselves. These freedoms and powers derive from the recognition of a few fundamental inalienable and sacrosanct rights termed human rights.

I am not avoiding the objection which could be raised over the fact that the recognition of the individual as a holder of rights did not await the Copernican revolution of natural law. The primacy of right (*jus*) over obligation is typical of Roman law as it was developed by jurists in the classical era. As everyone can see for themselves, these rights were due to the individual as an economic agent, as a holder of rights over property with power to exchange goods with economic agents enjoying the same power. The turning-point, which I referred to and which is fundamental to the recognition of human rights, occurred when the sphere of interpersonal economic relationships was extended to the power relationships between the sovereign and his subjects, with the creation of the so-called subjective public rights which typify the constitutional state. It is with the birth of the constitutional state that there is the final transition from the sovereign's point of view to that of the citizen. In the despotic state, the individual has duties not rights. In the absolutist state, individuals can claim private rights in relation to the sovereign. In the constitutional state, the individual in relation to the state enjoys not only private rights but also public rights. The constitutional state is a citizens' state.

5. Since its first appearance in the political thought of the seventeenth and eighteenth centuries, the doctrine of human rights has made considerable headway, albeit among conflicts, confutations and restrictions. Although the ultimate goal of a society of free and equal citizens which reproduces the hypothetical state of nature has not been achieved, precisely because such a goal is utopian, various stages have been completed and it would not be so easy to turn back.

Apart from the positivization, generalization and internationalization which I spoke of at the beginning, a new trend has appeared in recent years which could be called *specification*, which involves a gradual but increasingly marked transition towards a further definition of the persons enjoying the rights. The same thing is happening in relation to the right-holder as previously occurred with the abstract idea of freedom, which has been gradually broken down into individual concrete freedoms (of conscience, of thought, of the press, of assembly, of association) in an uninterrupted and still continuing process. Suffice it to consider the safeguards for one's own image against the invasiveness of the means of reproduction and distribution in the outside world, or the safeguards for confidentiality against the increased ability of public bodies to store information on an individual's private life. Equally, in relation to abstract man whose initial specification was 'citizen' (in the sense that the citizen could be attributed further rights in relation to man in general), there has arisen a need to respond more specifically to the question: which man or which citizen?

This specification has occurred both in relation to gender, the various stages in one's life, and taking into account the difference between the normal and exceptional states of human existence. As far as gender is concerned, there has been an increasing recogni tion of the specific differences between women and men. As far as the stages of one's life are concerned, there has been a gradual differentiation of the rights of children and the rights of old people from those of working age. In relation to normal and exceptional states, the need has arisen to recognize special rights for the sick, the handicapped, the mentally ill, and so on.

A glance through the documents approved in recent decades demonstrates this innovation. I refer, for example, to the Declaration of the Rights of Children (1959), the Declaration on the Elimination of Discrimination against Women (1967) and the Declaration of the Rights of the Mentally Ill (1971). As far as the rights of old people are concerned, there are various documents which came out after the World Assembly held in Vienna from 26 July to 6 August 1982 whose agenda included the question of new international programmes to guarantee social and economic security for old people, whose numbers are rising.

Looking beyond our own times, we can already identify the extension to the right to life for future generations whose survival is threatened by the exponential growth in ever more destructive weapons, and to new subjects, such as animals which common morality has always considered as objects or, at the very most, passive subjects without any rights. Of course all these new perspectives are part of what at the beginning I called the prophetic history of humanity, which historians refuse to recognize because they only allow themselves purely conjectural predictions and reject prophecy as inappropriate to their tasks.

Coming down from the ideal plain to the real, it is one thing to discuss human rights, new and increasingly extensive rights, and justify them with persuasive arguments; but it is quite another to ensure their effective protection. On this point, it would be worth repeating this observation: as the demands gradually multiply, so their fulfilment becomes increasingly difficult. As is well known, it is more difficult to protect social rights than libertarian rights. We are all equally aware that international protection is more difficult than protection within a state, particularly a constitutional state. One could find countless examples of the contrast between solemn declarations and their implementation, between the grandiloquence of the promises and the wretchedness of what is actually accomplished. Given that I have interpreted the vastness of current debate on human rights as a sign of humanity's moral progress, it would not be out of place to repeat that this moral growth has to be measured in deeds not words. The road to hell is paved with good intentions.

Let me conclude. I started by stating that to view things in terms of philosophy of history is to address the question of the meaning of history. But does history have a meaning within itself? By history I mean the sequence of events which is narrated by historians. History only has the meaning we attribute to it on each occasion according to our hopes and desires. Therefore it does not have a single meaning. It seemed to me when reflecting on human rights that I could detect humanity's moral progress. But is this the only meaning? When I reflect upon other aspects of our times, such as the bewilderingly rapid arms race which endangers the very life of the planet, I am obliged to give a completely different interpretation.

I started with Kant, and with Kant I shall end. Human progress was not a necessity for Kant, it was only a possibility. He reproached 'politicians' for having no faith in the virtue and force of moral motivation, and for constantly repeating: 'The world will always be the same as it has been up till now'. He commented that by adopting this attitude they were fulfilling their own prediction of history's inertia and monotonous repetition. Thus they artfully delay the means by which they could ensure progress towards a better world.

We have already delayed too much for the great aspirations of well-intentioned people. Do not let us further increase this delay with our despair, lethargy and scepticism. We have no time to waste.

Notes

1 G. Peces-Barba (ed.), *Derecho positivo de los derechos humanos* (Madrid: Editorial Debate, 1987), pp. 13–14.
2 K. Jaspers, *The Origin and Goal of History*, trans. M. Bullock (London: Routledge & Kegan Paul, 1953).

3 I. Kant, 'A Renewed Attempt to Answer the Question: "Is the Human Race Continually Improving?" ', in *Political Writings*, ed. Hans Reis, trans. H B Nisbet (Cambridge: Cambridge University Press, 1991), p. 187.

4 J.-J. Rousseau, *The Social Contract*, trans. G.D.H. Cole (London: Dent, 1973), II, 7, p. 194.

5 Plato, *The Laws*, trans. T.J. Saunders (Harmondsworth: Penguin Books, 1975), p. 45, bk. I, 624a.

6 C. Montesquieu, *The Spirit of the Laws*, ed. and trans. A.H. Cohler, B.A. Miller and H.S. Stone (Cambridge: Cambridge University Press, 1989), p. 5.

7 J. Locke, *The Second Treatise on Civil Government*, II, 4, ed. J.W. Gough (Oxford: Basil Blackwell, 1946), p. 4.

8 E. Burke, *Speech on the Economic Reform* (1780), in *Works* (London: World Classics, 1906), vol. II, p. 357. Quoted in S. Lukes, *Individualism* (Oxford: Blackwell, 1985), p. 3.

9 F.R. Lamennais, *Des progrès de la révolution et de la guerre contre l'église* (1829), in *œvres complètes* (Paris: n. pub., 1836–7), vol. XI, pp. 17–18. Quoted in Lukes, *Individualism*, p. 7.

4 Human Rights and Society

In a general discussion of human rights, the first thing is to separate theory and practice, or rather to realize right from the beginning that theory and practice travel along two different tracks and at very different speeds. What I am saying is that over the last few years there has been a great deal more discussion about human rights among scholars, philosophers, jurists, sociologists and politicians than there has been success in obtaining their recognition and protection – that is to say, transforming noble but vague aspirations and just but weak demands into legally established rights.

Bearing in mind this distinction between two levels which must not be confused, it can be argued that since the war the theory and practice of human rights (more the theory than the practice) have essentially developed in two directions: towards their universalization and their proliferation.

I will not go into universalization here, as in my opinion it is less relevant to the sociology of law, and also because the subject has been widely dealt with in the doctrine of international law which correctly sees this process as the starting point for a profound transformation of the law of 'peoples', as it has been called for centuries, into a law of 'individuals' – that is to say, single individuals who are being transformed from citizens of a single state into citizens of the world through the potential acquisition of the right to take legal action against their own states.

I shall focus on the second process, proliferation, because it lends itself to certain reflections on the relationship between human rights and society, the social origins of human rights, and the close connection between social change and the creation of new rights, matters which I think are of greater interest to a meeting of sociologists of law, whose specific task is to reflect upon the law as a social phenomenon.

There can be no doubt that human rights are at least partly a social phenomenon. They can be looked at from a philosophical, legal or economic point of view, and there is also room for the sociological approach, which is precisely that of legal sociology.

This proliferation has occurred in three ways: a) because of the increase in the number of assets considered worthy of protection; b) because a few typical rights have been extended to entities other than human beings; c) because human beings themselves are no longer considered a generic entity or abstract man, but are seen in their specific or concrete situation in society: as a child, old person, sick person, etc. Basically more assets, subjects and 'status' for the single individual. Needless to say these three processes are interdependent: the recognition of new rights *of* (where 'of' indicates the subject) nearly always involves an increase in rights *to* (where 'to' indicates the object). It also hardly needs pointing out that all three causes of this spiralling proliferation of human rights make it increasingly clear that one must refer to a specific social context.

The first process has already moved on from the libertarian rights or so-called negative rights of religion, thought, press, etc., to political and social rights which require direct intervention by the state. The second process has moved on from the consideration of the human individual as a single entity taken on its own, in other words the 'person' who was initially attributed natural (or moral rights), to entities other than the individual, such as the family, ethnic and religious minorities, or all humanity in the current debate among moral philosophers on the right of future generations to survival. Apart from human individuals taken singularly or within the real or ideal communities which represent them, there are now even categories outside humanity, such as animals. The ecological movements are putting forward what is almost a right of nature to be respected and not exploited, where the words 'respect' and 'exploitation' are used in exactly the same way as they have traditionally been used for the definition and justification of human rights.

The third process has moved on from the generic human being or the human being per se, to the specific human being, or the human being in the specificity of differing social *status*, on the basis of various criteria for differentiation: sex, age, physical conditions, each of which reveals specific differences which do not allow equal treatment and equal protection. Women are different from men, children from adults, adults of working age from old people, the healthy from the sick, the temporarily sick from the chronically sick, the mentally ill from the other sick, the physically normal from the handicapped, and so on. Suffice it to glance through successive international charters of rights over the last forty years to get an idea of this phenomenon: the Convention on the Political Rights of Women in 1952, the Declaration of the Rights of Children in 1959, the Declaration of the Rights of the Mentally Handicapped in 1971, the Declaration of the Rights of Handicapped Persons in 1975, and the first World Assembly on the Rights of Old People held in Vienna in 1982, which put forward a plan of action which was approved by a resolution of the General Assembly of the United Nations on 3 December.

Of course this proliferation through specification has mainly occurred in the field of social rights. The rights of negative freedom, the first rights to be recognized and protected, are valid for the abstract man. Predictably they first appeared as the rights of Man. Religious freedom, once it has been established, was extended to everyone, even though at the beginning it was not granted to some confessions or to atheists, but they were exceptions which had to be justified. It was the same for freedom of thought. Libertarian rights develop along with the principle of equal treatment. The principle that all men are equal is valid for libertarian rights. In Locke's state of nature, which was the great inspiration for declarations of human rights, all men are equal, where 'equality' means equal in the enjoyment of freedom, that no individual can have more freedom than another. This type of equality is proclaimed, for example, in Article I of the Universal Declaration with the statement: 'Men have equal right to liberty', 'Men have right to equal freedom'. These are formulas based on the same principle according to which all discrimination between one person and another, and between one group and another, should be eliminated, as can be read in Article 3 of the Italian Constitution which, after having stated that all men have 'equal social dignity', specifies that they are equal 'before the law, irrespective of sex, race, language, religion, political opinions and personal or social conditions'. The same principle is even more explicit in Article 2, § 1 of the Universal Declaration, according to which 'every individual is due all the rights and all the liberties proclaimed in this declaration, without any distinction for reasons of colour, sex, language, religion, political or any other type of opinion, national or social origin, wealth, birth or other condition'.

This universality, lack of distinction or non-discrimination in the attribution and enjoyment of libertarian rights is not applicable to social rights, nor indeed to political rights, for which individuals are only generically but not specifically equal. Political and social rights still differ considerably and intrinsically from one individual to another, or rather from one group of individuals to another. For centuries only men, and not all men, had the right to vote. Today minors still do not have the vote, and it is unlikely that they will obtain it in the near future. This means that the affirmation and recognition of political rights can only acknowledge the differences which justify an unequal treatment. This is even more the case in the field of social rights. It is only in a general and rhetorical sense that one can state that everyone is equal in relation to the three fundamental social rights to work, education and health, while it can realistically be said that everyone is equal in the enjoyment of negative freedoms. The reason why it cannot be said is that the attribution of social rights must take into account specific differences which are important in distinguishing one individual from another, or rather one group of individuals from another. The passage I just referred to from Article 3 of the Italian Constitution which stated that all citizens are equal irrespective of 'personal or social conditions' is not true in relation to social rights, because certain personal and social conditions are particularly relevant to the allocation of these rights. As far as work is concerned, there are differences in age and sex; as far as education is concerned, there are differences between normal and abnormal children; and as far as health is concerned, there are differences between adults of working age and old people.

I do not intend to carry these arguments through to their ultimate conclusions. I merely wish to establish that equality and distinction differ in importance according to whether one is discussing libertarian or social rights. This is also the reason why the proliferation I mentioned earlier has occurred more in the field of social rights than in the field of libertarian rights, because it was through the recognition of social rights that next to abstract man, the indeterminate citizen, there have appeared other holders of rights unknown to the declarations of libertarian rights: women, children, the old, the very old, the sick, the mentally ill, and so on.

It hardly needs to be said that, apart from the proliferation of human rights, the recognition of social rights poses problems which are considerably more difficult to resolve in terms of the 'praxis' I spoke of earlier. This is because the protection of these social rights requires active intervention from the state which is not required for the protection of libertarian rights, and has produced an organization of public services that has brought with it a new form of state, the welfare state. While libertarian rights originate from the excessive power of the state and therefore limit its power, social rights require practical implementation. Thus their transition from a purely verbal declaration to their effective protection involves an increase in the powers of the state. 'Power' has both a positive and a negative connotation according to its context, just like any other political term, including 'freedom'. The exercise of power can be considered beneficial or harmful according to the historical context and the different points of view used in the consideration of these contexts. It is not the case that an increase in freedom is always a good thing, and an increase in power is always a bad thing.

I have been emphasizing the proliferation of human rights as a feature of the current phase in the development of the theory and practice of these rights, because in my opinion there is no better way of demonstrating the link between social change and change in the theory and practice of human rights, and therefore to shed light on the most interesting and fruitful aspect of human rights as studied by legal sociologists.

I commence with Renato Treves' distinction between the two essential tasks of the sociology of law: the investigation of the law's role in social change, and therefore the entire range of specific human rights, a task which could be summarized by the term 'law within society'; and analysis of the extent to which legal norms are applied within a given society, including the extent of their application within individual states and within the overall international system, in relation to human rights, a task which can be summarized by the term 'society within the law'. Both tasks are very topical and can be specifically applied to any constitution which includes the recognition and protection of human rights.

The reason why we can speak of the task for the sociology of law in relation to the question of human rights, a task which distinguishes the sociology of law from the philosophy of law, the general theory of law and jurisprudence, is precisely because the birth and now the growth of human rights is closely connected to the transformation of society. This is clearly shown by the link between the proliferation of human rights and social development. Sociology in general and sociology of law in particular are therefore in the best position to make a special contribution to the understanding of the problem.

The doctrine of human rights originated from the philosophy of natural law, based on the theory of a state of nature where human rights were few and fundamental. It was used to justify the existence of rights inherently belonging to man independent of the state, such as the right to life and survival, the right to property and the right to liberty, which in turn includes a few liberties which are essentially negative liberties. Kant's theory can be considered the conclusion of this first stage in the history of human rights which culminated with the first declarations by holders of governmental power and therefore *cum imperio* (with authority), and no longer just by philosophers and therefore *sine imperio* (without authority). The theory he put forward was that man in the state of nature had a single right, the right to liberty as 'independence from all constrictions imposed by another will', because this covers all other rights, including the right of equality.

The hypothesis of a state of nature, existing before the state and for some writers before society, was an attempt to justify rationally, or to rationalize, firstly the demands for freedom of conscience against any form of coercion on belief which became widespread during the religious wars, and secondly the demands for civil liberties against any form of despotism during the age which commenced with the English Revolution and continued through to the American and French Revolutions. The state of nature was a purely doctrinal fiction which served to justify demands for freedom as rights inherent in the very nature of man, and as such inviolable for those in power, inalienable for those who hold the rights and indefeasible, irrespective of the period over which they had been violated or alienated. These demands for freedom came from those who were struggling against the dogmatism of the churches and the authoritarianism of the states. The demands for these rights were born in a reality marked by the conflicts and movements which nurtured them. If one wants to understand the reasons for these conflicts and movements, one must look for them not in the theory of the state of nature but in the social reality of the time and changes which these conflicts occasionally brought about.

This need to move from the rational hypothesis to the analysis of real societies and their histories is even more relevant now that demands from below calling for greater protection of individuals and groups have increased enormously and continue to increase. These are demands which go far beyond freedom *from* and freedom *of*, and to justify them the abstract theory of a simple and primitive state of nature where man lived with a few essential needs would have no persuasive power at all, and therefore no theoretical or practical usefulness. The fact that the list of these rights is growing continuously not only demonstrates that the initial basis for the state of nature is no longer plausible, but should also suggest to us that the social relations which gave rise to these demands must be equally complex, and that the so-called fundamental rights of life, liberty and property are no longer sufficient for life and survival in this new society.

Convincingly, there are no current charters of rights which do not recognize the right to education, and this broadens as society develops: first primary education, then secondary education, and very gradually university education as well. As far as I know, none of the better-known descriptions of the state of nature mentioned such a right. The truth is that this right did not arise in the state of nature, because it had not yet emerged in the society at the time when the doctrines of natural law were being formulated, when the fundamental demands on the powerful coming from that society were principally demands for freedom from the church and state, and not yet benefits like education, which could only be expressed by a more economically and socially developed society. They were demands whose primary purpose was to place limitations on oppressive powers, so the theory of a pre-state existence or a state free from powers above the individual, such as churches and governments, corresponded perfectly to the arguments for reducing their jurisdiction to a minimum and expanding the area of individual liberty. Conversely, the theory of man as a political animal, which goes back to Aristotle, had been used for centuries to justify the paternalistic state, and, in its crudest form, despotism, in which the individual does not naturally possess any rights because, like a child, he would not be able to use them for the common good or even for his own benefit. It was no coincidence that Locke's direct adversary was the most rigid supporter of the patriarchal state, and that the supporter of the right of liberty as a fundamental right was at the same time the most coherent adversary of patriarchy, a form of government which treats its subjects as eternal minors.

While the relationship between social change and the birth of libertarian rights is less clear and might have sustained the theory that the demand for civil liberties was founded on the existence of natural rights inherent to man independent of any historical considerations, the relationship between the birth and growth of social rights on the one hand and the transformation of society on the other is very clear indeed. The proof is that demands for social rights have become more numerous as the transformation of society has become more rapid and profound. One should also remember that demands which call on public intervention and the provision of social services by the state can only be satisfied by a certain level of economic and technological development, and theory itself is affected by the emergence of new demands which would have been unpredictable and impracticable before these transformations and innovations had occurred. This is a further confirmation of the social nature of these rights, of their non-naturalness.

A very topical example is the demand for greater protection for old people which could not have occurred if there had not been an increase in the number of old people and their longevity – both effects of changes in social relations and advances in medicine. And then there are the ecological movements and the demands for greater protection of nature, which involve a ban on the abuse or improper use of natural resources essential to man. Besides, even the sphere of libertarian rights has been changing and expanding because of technical innovation in the transmission and distribution of ideas and images, and their possible abuse, which would have been inconceivable when they were technically difficult or impossible. This means that the link between social change and change in the theory and practice of fundamental rights has always existed, and the birth of social rights has only made this more evident, so evident that it can no longer be ignored. In a society in which only property owners held active citizenship, it was a foregone conclusion that the right to property was raised to the status of a fundamental right, just as in countries of the first industrial revolution the right to work was made a fundamental right, once the workers' movements entered the scene. The demand that the right to work should be a fundamental right, as generally recognized by contemporary declarations of rights, had the same good reasons as the earlier demand that the right of property be a natural right. These good reasons were rooted in the nature of the power relations which governed the society that generated them, and therefore in the specific, historically determined nature of those societies.

The task of legal sociologists in relation to the other fundamental question, the application of legal norms, is vast and even more important. This phenomenon is called *implementation*. The field of human rights, or more precisely the norms which proclaim, recognize, define and assign human rights, is certainly the one with the greatest difference between the norm and its actual application. This is particularly true of the field of social rights. Thus in the Italian Constitution the norms which refer to social rights are modestly called 'programmatic'. Have we ever asked ourselves what kind of laws are these which do not command, prohibit and consent *hic et nunc* (in this time and place), but command, prohibit and consent in some undefined future with no particular deadline? And above all, have we ever wondered what kind of rights these laws define? Can we properly call something a right if its recognition and effective protection are postponed *sine die* and are entrusted to the commitment of people whose only obligation to implement the 'programme' is moral, or at the most political? Isn't the difference between these self-proclaimed rights and rights in the proper sense of the term great enough to make it incorrect or at least not very helpful to use the same word for both? Apart from anything else, the great majority of norms on human rights, as issued by international bodies, are not even programmatic norms like those in a national constitution concerning social rights, or they are not until they are ratified by individual states. Professor Evan's research on the number of ratifications of the two international conventions on human rights by member states of the United Nations is much more instructive on this point: it shows that only two-fifths of the states have ratified them, and there are large differences between the states of the first, second and third worlds. While charters of rights remain solely within the ambit of the international system which proclaims them, they are more expressions of good intentions than charters of rights in the strict sense of the term. At the very most they can be considered general plans of action directed towards an undefined and uncertain future, with no serious guarantees of implementation other than the good will of states and no support other than the pressure of international public opinion or non-state agencies like Amnesty International.

This is not the proper place to tackle the question of the various meanings of the term 'right', and the related disputes which are largely superficial, and cannot be avoided when human rights are precisely the matter under discussion. Whether one approaches the problem through the classical distinction between natural rights and positive rights, or the distinction more commonly used in Anglo-Saxon philosophy between *moral rights* and *legal rights*, one cannot help immediately detecting a change in the meaning of the word 'right' between the first and the second term. It is a question of whether it is appropriate to use the term 'right' not only in the second but also in the first instance. I share the concern of those for whom applying the word 'rights' to demands for what are at best future rights, means creating expectations which can never be satisfied among people who use the word 'right' according to its current meaning of an expectation which can be satisfied because it is protected.

Out of prudence I have always used the word 'demands' rather than 'rights' throughout my report, when referring to rights which are not recognized constitutionally, and are therefore mere aspirations for future (positive) rights, even if justified with plausible arguments. I could have used the term 'claim' which belongs to legal terminology and is often used in discussions on the nature of human rights, but in my opinion it is still too forceful. Naturally, I have nothing against applying the term 'rights' to demands for future rights, as long as one avoids the confusion between a demand for the future protection of a certain asset however well argued and the actual protection of this asset which you can obtain by recourse to a court of justice authorized to redress the grievance and in some cases punish the guilty party. I would suggest to those who do not wish to renounce the word 'right' for reasoned demands for future protection that they should distinguish between a right in a weak sense and a right in a strong sense.

'Right' is a deontic concept and therefore a normative term, in other words part of a language which deals with norms. The existence of a right, both in the weak sense and the strong one, always implies the existence of a normative system, where 'existence' can be interpreted equally as the purely external reality of a historical or current right or the recognition of a set of norms as a guide to one's own actions. The concept of right has a related concept of duty. Just as there cannot be a father without a son, so there cannot be a right without a duty, or vice versa. The old idea that there were duties without corresponding rights, such as the duty to be charitable, arose from the failure to recognize the beneficiary as the holder of a right. This does not mean that the duty to be charitable was not an obligation to God or one's own conscience, which were the true holders of the right in relation to the benefactor, and not the beneficiary him- or herself. One can talk of moral rights only in the context of a moral normative system, where the reason for the duties is not an authority backed by coercive force, but God, one's own conscience or social pressure, according to various moral theories. One can only talk of natural rights by assuming, as the proponents of natural law did, that the existence of a system of natural laws which, like all laws, designate rights and duties, and these rights and duties can be derived from the observation of human nature and the natural code of order, just as positive rights can be deduced from the study of a code of positive laws established by an authority competent to impose its own commands. Moral duties, natural duties, positive duties and relative duties belong to different normative systems. Terms such as duty and right must be put into a normative context in order to have meaning, irrespective of the nature of that context. But as far as positive rights are concerned, natural rights are only demands motivated by historical and rational arguments in order to be accepted into an effective legal system. From the point of view of a legal system, the so-called moral or natural rights are not properly speaking rights at all: they are only needs which could be established and transformed into rights in a new normative system characterized by a different manner of protecting rights. The transformation from one set of laws to another is also determined by the social context and is in no way predetermined.

The advocates of natural law will object that there are absolute natural or moral rights, which as such are also rights in every other historical and positive normative system. But a statement of this kind is contradicted by the variety of natural and moral codes which are proposed, and by common usage which does not accept as 'rights' the majority of the demands and claims which have established themselves doctrinally or are even supported by a large and authoritative section of public opinion, until they are sanctioned by a positive legal system. For example, before women obtained the right to vote in different legal systems, it was arguable that one could correctly speak of the natural or moral right of women to vote when the reasons for not recognizing this right were both natural (women were not naturally independent) and moral (women are too emotive to be able to express an opinion on a law which must be rationally argued). It is doubtful that there was a right to conscientious objection before this was recognized. What is the point in asserting a natural or moral right to conscientious objection, where there is no legal recognition? Is it not sufficient to say that there are good reasons for this demand being approved. It is difficult to see the sense in claiming that women had a right to abortion, before this aspiration was accepted and recognized by civil legislation on the basis of reasons which were partly historically and socially determined, such as the increasing number of working women and the danger which overpopulation poses for humanity – reasons which therefore do not have absolute validity.

I could go on. This argument is particularly important in relation to human rights, which have undergone a historic transformation from a system of rights in the weak sense, in that they were part of a code of natural and moral norms, to a system of rights in the strong sense, as legal systems within the nation states. Today with the various international charters of rights, we are moving from a strong system, that of the non-despotic nation state to a weaker international system, where the rights proclaimed are almost exclusively sustained by social pressure, as generally occurs with moral codes, and they are repeatedly violated, usually without the violations being punished and there being no response other than moral censure. The international system lacks some of the necessary conditions for the transformation of rights in the weak sense into rights in the strong sense: (a) the recognition and protection of claims and demands contained in the declarations issued by international bodies and agencies being considered a necessary condition for a state's membership of the international community; and (b) a common international authority strong enough to prevent and suppress the violation of proclaimed rights.

I originally wrote this essay for a conference on the sociology of law. As sociologists of law can observe the interrelation between legal systems and social systems in their professional life, it seemed the perfect opportunity to denounce the abuse or rather the deceitful use which is made of the term 'right' in the declarations of this or that human right in the international community. Given that the people sitting around the table at international meetings are politicians, diplomats, jurists and experts in general, there must be an element of hypocrisy and they cannot ignore the fact that the matters under discussion are purely and simply proposals or directives for future legislation. They must be aware that the charters proclaimed at the end of these meetings are not really charters of rights, such as those which have introduced national constitutions since the end of the eighteenth century, nor are they 'bills of rights', to use the expression with which human rights first appeared on the historical stage. Instead they are documents relating to what will or should be rights in a not-too-distant future, when the individual states have recognized them or the international system has established the organs and powers necessary to impose them, should they be violated. A right is one thing, and the promise of a right is another. A current right is one thing, and a potential right is another. Having an existing recognized and protected right is a very different thing from having a right which ought to exist, but which has to be transformed from a matter for discussion by an assembly of experts into a decision by a legislative body provided with some powers of coercion in order to make the leap from 'should be existing' to 'actually existing'.

I started by asserting the enormous difference between the widespread theoretical debate on human rights and the limitations on their effective protection in the individual states and the international system. This void can only be filled by political forces, but sociologists of law are amongst the scholars of legal disciplines best placed to report on that void, explain its reasons, and thus assist in reducing it.

5 Human Rights Today

In one of my writings on human rights, I resurrected Kant's idea of prophetic history to show how the importance of human rights in current political debate is a *sign of the times*.[1] While history written by historians attempts to find out about the past, using accounts and conjectures, and makes cautious predictions about the future which almost always turn out to be wrong, using hypotheses in the form 'if, then . . .', prophetic history does not predict but foretells the future by extracting the single most extraordinary event from the other events of its time, and interpreting that event as a particularly indicative sign of a trend in humanity towards a certain end, whether that end is desired or opposed. I therefore argued that the current increasingly widespread debate on human rights, which has been put on the agenda of the most authoritative international bodies, could be interpreted as a 'premonitory sign', perhaps the only one, of what Kant termed the human tendency to improve.

When I wrote these words, I did not know the text of the document produced by the Papal Commission 'Iustitia et Pax', entitled *The Church and Human Rights*, which commenced with the statement:

The dynamic development of the faith is continuously driving God's people to read the *signs of the times* carefully and proficiently. In the current era, the increasing attention paid in every part of the world to human rights is one of the various signs of the times which cannot be considered of secondary importance, both because of the increasingly profound and sensitive awareness of such rights at individual and community level, and because of the continuous and distressing proliferation of their violations.[2]

The sign of the times is not Hegel's 'spirit of the age' which, interlinked with the 'spirit of the people', forms the 'spirit of the world'. The spirit of the times is used to interpret the present, while the sign of the times is used for a reckless, indiscrete, uncertain but hopeful glance at the future.

The signs of the time are unpropitious as well as propitious. Never has there been such a plethora of prophets of doom as there is today: atomic annihilation, the second death as it has been called, the progressive and relentless destruction of the conditions which allow life on earth, moral nihilism and the 'overturning of all values'. The century which is now drawing to a close started with the idea of decline or decadence. Partly at the suggestion of barely understood scientific theories the use of the much stronger word 'catastrophe' is now becoming increasingly widespread: atomic catastrophe, ecological catastrophe and moral catastrophe. Until recently we were happy with Kant's metaphor of man as a twisted piece of wood. In one of the most fascinating essays of this rigorous critic of reason, *Idea for a Universal History with a Cosmopolitan Intent*, Kant wondered whether something completely straight could come out of the twisted piece of wood that was man. But Kant himself believed that humanity would gradually draw nearer to the ideal of 'straightness' through 'a correct conception of the nature of a possible constitution, great experience tested in many affairs of the world, and above all else a good will prepared to accept the findings of this experience'.[3] He defined the concept of the future which considered the human condition to be getting continually worse as 'terroristic', and wrote that 'a process of deterioration in the human race cannot go on indefinitely, for mankind would wear itself out after a certain point had been reached'.[4] And yet it is precisely this rush towards self-destruction which emerges in the catastrophic visions of today. According to one of the most fearless and melancholic proponents of the terroristic concept of history, man is a 'mistaken animal',[5] but it should be emphasized that he is not guilty, for that is the old familiar story of man being guilty but redeemable, and possibly already redeemed without his knowledge. A twisted piece of wood can be straightened, but for this bitter interpreter of our age, man is incorrigible.

Yet never before has the idea of human rights spread so quickly, especially since the Second World War, which certainly was a catastrophe. I do not know whether this idea is ambitious, sublime, merely consolatory, or naively hopeful, but it invites us to cancel the image of the twisted piece of wood or the mistaken animal, and no longer depicts the contradictory and ambiguous being called man solely in terms of his wretchedness, but also in terms of his potential grandeur.

In principle, the enormous importance of the human rights question derives from the fact that it is closely linked to two fundamental problems of our times: democracy and peace. The recognition and protection of human rights are the foundations on which democratic constitutions are built, and at the same time peace is the precondition for the effective protection of human rights within individual states and the international system. The old adage *'inter arma silent leges'* ('whenever weapons clash, the laws fall silent') is still true and we have recently experienced it again. Today we are more convinced than ever that the ideal of perpetual peace can only be pursued through a progressive democratization of the international system, and this democratization cannot be separated from the gradual and increasingly effective protection of human rights at a higher level than the individual state. Human rights, democracy and peace are the three elements necessary for this historic movement. There is no democracy without the recognition and effective protection of human rights; without democracy the minimum conditions do not exist for the peaceful resolution of conflicts between individuals, between groups and between the large collectivities called states which traditionally have been so intractable and tendentially autocratic, even when they are democratic with their own citizens.

It is worth remembering that the Universal Declaration of Human Rights starts by stating that 'the recognition of the innate dignity of all members of the human family and their equal and inalienable rights constitutes the foundation for freedom, justice and peace in the world', and these words refer directly back to the UN statute which follows a restatement of faith in the fundamental human rights with the declaration that it is necessary 'to save future generations from the scourge of war'.

I read in a recent work, *Etica y derechos humanos* that: 'There can be no doubt that human rights are one of the greatest inventions of our civilization.'[6] If the word 'invention' seems a little too strong, one could say 'innovation', using the term 'innovation' in the same way as Hegel when he said that the biblical saying 'nothing new under the sun' was not true for the sun of the Spirit, because its path never repeats itself, but is the ever-changing manifestation of the spirit which is essentially progress.[7]

While it is true that the universality of human nature is an ancient concept, which suddenly appeared in Western history with the advent of Christianity, the transformation of this philosophical idea of the universality of human nature into a political institution (this is where the 'innovation' lies), into different and in a sense revolutionary ways of regulating relationships between governments and the governed, only occurs in the modern age, through the theory of natural law, and it found its first significant political expression in the declarations of rights at the end of the eighteenth century. Whether one calls it an invention or an innovation, when declarations are no longer just found in philosophical texts such as Locke's *Second Treatise on Civil Government*, but political documents such as the Declaration of Rights of Virginia (1778) which reads: 'All men are by nature equally free, and have some inherent rights of which they cannot deprive their descendants through convention on entering society', we have to admit that in that moment a new form of political rule has been created, and I mean literally one without precedent, one which is not a government of laws, which Aristotle praised, as opposed to a government of men, but a government of men and laws together, of men who make laws and laws which are restricted by pre-existing individual rights which the laws themselves cannot infringe. In a word, the modern liberal state evolved through internal development into the democratic state without problems of continuity.

The innovation, which has led me on other occasions to speak in Kantian terms of a full-blown Copernican revolution in the manner of interpreting political relations, operates on two levels. Stating that man has rights which pre-existed the creation of the state (i.e. a power which is assigned the task of taking collective decisions, which once they have been taken, must be obeyed by everyone who makes up that collectivity) means overturning the traditional concept of politics from at least two points of view: firstly, by contrasting man, men and individuals taken singly, with society, civic organization, and in particular that civic organization which is termed *res publica* or the state, in other words to the totality which for so long had been considered superior to its parts; secondly, by believing that rights come before duties in moral and legal relations, contrary to the long tradition which continued through classical works, and went from Cicero's *De officiis* to Pufendorf's *De officio hominis et civis* and then to Mazzini's *Doveri dell'uomo*.

As far as the first inversion is concerned, the organic concept which had been dominant for centuries and is still reflected in such political terms as 'political bodies' and state 'organs', was finally abandoned when political relations were considered no longer from the government's point of view but from that of the governed, no longer from the top downwards but from the bottom upwards, while the 'bottom' is no longer the people as a collective body, but the citizens who combine with one another to form a general will. As far as the second inversion is concerned, the primacy of rights does not at all imply the elimination of duty, because rights and duties are correlated terms, and one cannot assert a right without at the same time asserting the duty of another to respect that right. Anyone who is at all familiar with the history of political thought, will have learnt that the study of politics has always put greater emphasis on the citizen's duties than his rights (suffice it to recall the fundamental question of so-called political obligations) and greater emphasis on the rights and powers of the sovereign than those of the citizen: in other words, it assigns a position of active agent in the relationship more to the sovereign than to the subjects.

Although I believe one must be very cautious when talking of turning-points, qualitative leaps, epoch-making upheavals, I would not hesitate to affirm that the proclamation of human rights has cut the course of human history in two, as far as the concept of political relations is concerned. To return to our initial expression, it is a sign of the times that this break with tradition is becoming clearer and irreversible through the convergence of the three main currents of modern political thought, liberalism, socialism and social Christianity, so that without contradicting themselves, they find themselves in general agreement. They converge, although they retain their own identity in the preference they show for some rights over others, and thus they create an increasingly complex system of fundamental rights. Their practical integration is often made difficult precisely because of the different source of doctrinal inspiration and the different aims which each wishes to obtain, but it still represents a goal to be achieved in the hoped-for unity of humankind.

Chronologically, first come the libertarian rights proposed by liberal thought, where liberty is understood in the negative sense of liberty used by modern thinkers, as opposed to liberty in the sense used by ancient and medieval thinkers, for whom a free republic meant either not dependent on a superior power, such as kingdom or empire, or popular in the sense of being governed by the citizens themselves or by a group of them, and not by a prince imposed or legitimized by laws of succession.

Social rights, in the form of public education and the provisions in favour of work for 'the able-bodied poor who have not been able to find work', first appeared in the first section of the French Constitution of 1791, and were restated in Articles 21 and 22 of the Declaration of Rights of June 1793. The right to work became one of the themes of the passionate but sterile debate in the French Constituent Assembly of 1848, although a slight trace of it can be found in Article VIII of the Preamble. In a more substantial form, social rights entered modern constitutional history with the Weimar Constitution. Although apparently contradictory, they are in fact complementary, and the best argument is the one that perceives them as an extension to libertarian rights, in the sense that social rights are a necessary condition for the effective implementation of libertarian rights. Libertarian rights can only be ensured by guaranteeing that everyone has a minimum of economic security which allows them to live in dignity.

As for social Christianity, the document produced by the Papal Commission 'Iustitia et Pax', which has already been referred to, recognizes in all honesty that support for human rights has 'not always' been 'constant' over the centuries, and especially in the last two centuries there have been 'difficulties', 'reservations' and sometimes 'reactions' by Catholics against the spread of human rights declarations proclaimed by liberals and the laity. It referred in particular to 'cautious, negative and occasionally hostile and censorious attitudes' by Pius VI, Pius VII and Gregory XVI.[8] However, a change can be observed which commenced with Leo XIII, especially with the encyclical *Rerum Novarum* of 1891, which emphasized, among other libertarian rights of the liberal tradition, the right to association with particular regard to workers' associations – a right which is the basis for the pluralism of pressure groups which distinguishes the modern democracy from the ancient one (which continued up to Rousseau). Among the social rights of the socialist tradition, it emphasized the right to work and its protection in various ways, such as the right to a fair wage, the right to an appropriate rest, the defence of women and children, and it called on the intervention of the state. A hundred years later, following various, well-known documents, encyclicals, Christmas messages such as those of Pius XII in 1942 and 1944, the Pastoral Constitution of the Second Vatican Council *Gaudium et Spes*, and Paul VI's famous message to the Secretary General of the UN, we have a new document dated the first of May of this year, the encyclical *Centesimus Annus*, which officially reaffirms the importance the church attributes to the recognition of human rights and, as has already been observed, paragraph 47 contains an enlightening 'charter of human rights', preceded by these words: 'The peoples who are reforming their legal systems should give democracy an authentic and solid foundation through the explicit recognition of human rights.' The first of these rights is the right to life, followed by the right to grow in a united family, the right to develop one's own intelligence and liberty in the search and knowledge of truth, the right to participate in work, the right to form a family freely, and finally the source of all the previous rights, the right to religious freedom.

Everyone can see that the list of these rights is very different from the rights listed in the charters of the French Revolution. The right to life which appears here as the first right to be defended, does not appear anywhere in the French charters. In the American charters, it nearly always appears in the form 'right to enjoy and defend life' next to the other libertarian rights. In order not to cloud the much hoped-for convergence towards a common end for the universal protection of human rights, this difference is often glossed over. But the difference is there, and undoubtedly has philosophical significance. On the one hand, priority is given to the protection of libertarian rights in their various manifestations, and on the other, priority is given to the right to life, from the moment life starts and therefore against abortion, until the moment life ends and therefore against euthanasia. In the tradition of natural law, the right to life is recognized, in the rudimentary form argued by Hobbes, as the right not to be killed in the war of every man against every man in the state of nature, and therefore in the final analysis as the right to peace. In the Declaration of 1789, there are references to the protection of life in Articles 7, 8 and 9 which contain the fundamental principles of Habeas Corpus.

Today, the right to life has taken on a special importance, and all the more so, if one takes into account the fact that it is increasingly being extended to quality of life in the most recent international and church documents. One should not forget the association between the right to life and the right to liberty has already been made in the Universal Declaration of Human Rights, whose Article 3 states: 'Every individual has the right to life, liberty and security', and the European Charter of Human Rights whose Article I recognizes the right to life, even if the principle aim of the article is restricted to the defence of the individual from international killing, which means the protection of life in its fullness and not in the extreme cases of when it is about to start or about to finish.

Even though they were considered natural from the very beginning, human rights are not established for ever. One only has to think of the events surrounding the extension of political rights. For centuries it was not thought at all natural that women should vote. We can therefore say that human rights were not all established at the same time. However there seems little doubt that various traditions are coming together and forming together a single grand design for the defence of humanity, involving the three great assets: life, liberty and economic security.

Defence from what? An examination of history gives us a clear and simple reply: from Power, from every form of Power. The essential political relationship is the relationship between power and liberty. There is a close correlation between one and the other. The more you extend the power of one of two agents in a relationship, the more you limit the liberty of the other, and vice versa.

It is the form of power which distinguishes the current period from previous eras and strengthens the demands for new rights. The struggle for rights had to fight first against religious power, then political power and finally economic power. Today, the threats to life, liberty and security come from the increasing power of those who control scientific discovery and the applications that stem from it. We have entered an era which is called postmodern, and is characterized by enormous, precipitous and irreversible progress, the technological and consequently technocratic transformation of the world. Man has come a long way since Bacon said that science is power! The growth of knowledge has simply increased the possibility of man dominating nature and other men.

The new generation of rights, as they have been called, came after the rights which responded to the three ideal currents of our time, and they all arise from the danger posed to life, liberty and security by the growth in technological progress. Three examples at the heart of current debate will be sufficient: the right to live in an unpolluted environment, which has been the basis for the ecological movements that have shaken both individual countries and the international system; the right to privacy, which has been seriously endangered by the ability of public bodies to store information concerning a person's life, and hence control behaviour without the person knowing; and finally the right to the integrity of one's genetic heritage, which is already stirring up debate in international organizations; this goes far beyond the right to physical integrity proclaimed in Articles 2 and 3 of the European Convention on Human Rights and there will probably be fierce clashes between two opposite views of human nature.

In his speech on the theological foundations of human rights in November 1988, the Bishop of Roltenburg-Stuttgart, Walter Kasper, made a statement which could constitute the conclusion to my own essay: 'Human rights now constitute a new world ethos'.[9]

Naturally one should not forget that an ethos represents the world as it should be. The real world unfortunately presents a very different picture. The awareness of the importance in the long term of a policy which aims at the better formulation and protection of human rights is parallelled by their systematic violation in almost every country in the world, and in relations between one country and another, one race and another, the powerful and the weak, the rich and the poor, majorities and minorities, and the violent and the demoralized. The ethos of human rights shines out in the solemn declarations which almost always and everywhere remain a dead letter. The will to power has dominated and continues to dominate the course of history. The only reason for hope is that history experiences long time-scales and short time-scales. We should not deceive ourselves on this point: the history of human rights involves long time-scales. Besides, it has always been the case that the prophets of doom announce the imminent disaster which solicits vigilance, while the prophets of happier times look further ahead.

A distinguished contemporary historian referred to the sense of shortened time-scales which spreads in times of great upheavals, whether they are real or only feared, quoting the vision of the Travertine Sibyl: 'The years will be as short as months, the months as weeks, the weeks as days and the days as hours',[10] comparing it to the similar sense of shortened time-scales of the generation born in the technological era, for whom the transition from one phase of technical progress to another, which once would have required centuries, then required decades and now a few years. The two phenomena are different but the intention is the same: when you want to get somewhere quicker, you either shorten the route or lengthen your step.

Living time is not real time: sometimes it is more rapid, sometimes it is slower. The world transformations which we have lived through in the last few years, both the speed of technical progress and the collapse of a system of power which appeared extremely solid and indeed aspired to represent the future for the planet, evoke a twin sense of shortening and accelerating time-scales. We sometimes feel we are on the edge of the precipice and that catastrophe is imminent. Will we save ourselves? How will we save ourselves? Who will save us? Strangely, this sense of being pressured by events in relation to the future contrasts with the lengthening and slowing down of the past in relation to the origins of man which is put further and further back. As our memory loses itself in a remote past which increasingly recedes, so our imagination is fired with the idea of hastening towards the end. It is slightly the mood, which I am well-acquainted with, of the old man for whom the past is everything and the future is nothing. There would be little cause for joy if it were not for a great ideal like that of human rights, which completely reverses the sense of our time, because like every ideal it projects itself towards the long time-scale, and its advent cannot be the object of prediction but, as I said at the beginning, a presentiment.

In a view of history which has no place for reason, we have no choice but to place a wager – Hegel's times, in which he could tell his students in Berlin that reason governs the world, now seem very far off. If history is to lead to the realm of human rights rather than the realm of Big Brother, it will all be a question of commitment.

It is true that it is one thing to gamble and quite another to win. But it is also true that whoever gambles does so in the hope of winning. Hope is not enough to win, but if one does not have a little hope, then the game is lost before you even begin. If I were asked what is needed to create hope, I would repeat Kant's words which were quoted at the start: just concepts, great experience and above all good intentions.

Notes

1 'Kant and the French Revolution', a lecture I gave on the occasion of my honourary degree from Bologna University, which also appears in this volume, ch. 8.
2 *La chiesa e i diritti dell'uomo*, Working Document no. 1 (Rome: Vatican City, 1975), p. 1. This sentence comes from the beginning of the *Presentazione*, signed by Cardinal Maurice Roy, Chairman of the Papal Commission 'Iustitia et Pax'.
3 I. Kant, *Idea for a Universal History with a Cosmopolitan Purpose*, in *Political Writings* (Cambridge: Cambridge University Press, 1991), p. 47.
4 I. Kant, 'A Renewed Attempt to Answer the Question: "Is the Human Race Continually Improving" ', in *Political Writings*, p. 179.

5   I refer to E.M. Cioran, a moralist of Romanian origin who writes in French, see *Précis de décomposition* (Paris: n. pub., 1949) and *La Tentation d'exister* (Paris: n. pub., 1956).

6   C.S. Nino, *Etica y derechos humanos* (Buenos Aires: Paidos Studio, 1984), p. 13.

7   Hegel, 'Realization of Spirit in History', in *Lectures on the Philosophy of World History* (Cambridge: Cambridge University Press, 1975).

8   *La chiesa e i diritti dell'uomo* (Rome: Vatican City, 1975), p. 12. One of the recent issues of the international theological magazine *Concilium* (vol. XXVI, no. 2, 1990) was dedicated entirely to the question of human rights. An article by Leonard Sidler, *Diritti umani: una panoramica storica*, states that 'Even though our idea of human rights has only been developed in the modern era, its roots are in the twin pillars of Western civilization: the Judeo-Christian religion and the Graeco-Roman culture' (p. 31). An essay by Knut Walf, *Vangelo, diritto canonico e diritti umani*, admits that 'the Christian churches as a whole have had difficulty in recognizing human rights up till the middle of the twentieth century' (p. 58).

9   *Les Droits de l'homme et l'eglise*, published by the Papal Commission 'Iustitia et Pax' Vatican City, 1990, p. 49.

10 Reinhart Koselleck, *Accelerazione e secolarizzazione* (Naples: Istituto Suor Orsola Benincasa, 1989), p. 9.

Part II

6 The French Revolution and Human Rights

The Declaration of the Rights of Man and the Citizen was approved by the National Assembly on 26 August 1789. The debate which led to its approval took place over two periods. From 4 August it was discussed whether to proceed with a declaration of rights before proclaiming a constitution. The Assembly opted against those who considered it useless, those who considered it useful but to be postponed and those who considered it useful only if accompanied by a declaration of duties. Instead it decided almost unanimously in favour of a declaration of rights, which, according to one member influenced by Rousseau, amounted to the act of constituting a people. They decided to proclaim the declaration immediately and then proceed to the constitution. From 20 to 26 August, the text chosen by the Assembly was discussed and approved.

Commentators at the time and historians agree that this act represents one of those decisive moments which, at least symbolically, mark the end of one era and the start of the next, and therefore indicate a turning-point in the history of humankind. Georges Lefèbvre, a great historian of the Revolution, wrote: 'By proclaiming the liberty, equality and sovereignty of the people, the Declaration constituted the official demise of the Ancien Régime, destroyed by the Revolution.'[1] From the thousands of accounts of the meaning of this text left to us by nineteenth-century historians, I am going to choose one by Alexis de Tocqueville, the political writer who first questioned the way the revolution saw itself. Referring to the first phase of 1789, he describes it as 'a time of youthful enthusiasm, boldness, and generous and sincere passions, which in spite of all the errors, men would eternally recall, and which for some time yet would disturb the sleep of those who wish to enslave and corrupt other men'.[2]

Curiously, the same word 'enthusiasm' (a word which the rationalist Voltaire hated[3]) was used by Kant who, although condemning regicide as an abomination, wrote that this 'revolution . . . of a gifted people', which had also amassed 'miseries and atrocities', had, however, engendered 'a sympathy which borders almost on enthusiasm', and could only have been caused by 'a moral disposition within the human race'. Having defined enthusiasm as the 'passionate involvement in good', he then immediately explained that 'true enthusiasm is always directed exclusively towards the ideal, particularly towards that which is purely moral', and the moral cause of this enthusiasm was 'the right' of a people not to be prevented by other forces from establishing its own civil constitution which it believes to be good'.[4] Thus Kant directly related the aspect which he found to be positive in the Revolution to the right of a people to decide its own destiny by itself. According to Kant, this right was primarily revealed in the French Revolution. It was a right to liberty in one of the two principle meanings of the word, as self-determination, autonomy, and the ability to pass legislation affecting oneself, and also as the antithesis of all the forms of paternalistic and patriarchal power which typified the traditional despotic regimes. In a passage in *Perpetual Peace*, Kant defines liberty in the following manner: 'my external or rightful *freedom* should be defined as a warrant to obey no external laws except those to which I have given my consent'.[5] This definition clearly reflects the influence of Rousseau, who stated that 'obedience to a law which we prescribe to ourselves is liberty'.[6]

In spite of his disagreement with Kant's abstract idealism and his ostentatious superiority on behalf of Germans who did not need the Revolution because they had already had the Reformation, Hegel could not hide his admiration when he came to discuss the French Revolution in his lessons on the philosophy of history, and he also spoke of 'enthusiasm of the spirit' (*Enthusiasmus des Geistes*) which shook the world and spread across it, 'as though the true reconciliation between the divine and the world had occurred'.[7] He called it 'a splendid aurora', which caused 'all thinking beings to be in agreement in celebrating this epoch'. This metaphor expressed his own conviction that the Revolution had ushered in a new historical era, and he explicitly stated that in his opinion the wholly political purpose of the Declaration was to secure natural rights, the first of which was liberty, followed by equality before the law as a further specification of liberty.

The first, extensive, historically documented and philosophically argued defence of the Declaration was contained in the two parts of Thomas Paine's *Rights of Man*, which appeared in 1791 and 1792 respectively. The work was essentially a pamphlet against Edmund Burke, who in defence of the English Constitution had acrimoniously attacked the revolution from the very beginning and had said of human rights: 'We have not been drawn and trussed, in order that we may be filled, like stuffed birds in a museum, with chaff and rags, and paltry, blurred shreds of paper about the rights of man'.[8] For Burke, such sentiments as fear of God, respect for the king, and allegiance to Parliament are natural, while quite unnatural, indeed 'false and spurious' are those (with clear reference to natural rights) which teach us 'a servile, licentious, and abandoned insolence, to be our low sport for a few holidays, to make us perfectly fit for, and justly deserving of slavery, through the whole course of our lives'.[9] He explained that the English are attached to more natural sentiments, even if they are prejudices: 'We are afraid to put men to live and trade each on his own private stock of reason; because we suspect that this stock in each man is small, and that individuals would do better to avail themselves of the general bank and capital of nations, and of ages'.[10]

Paine's justification of human rights was based on religion, and at the time it could not have been otherwise. In his opinion, the foundations of human rights had to be found not within history, as Burke had done, but by transcending history and going back to the time when man was originally moulded by the hands of the Creator. History had proved nothing except our errors, which we had to free ourselves from. The first step can only be to reaffirm the unity of humankind which history has divided. Only thus can men realize that before they had civil rights produced by history, they had natural rights which were the foundation of all civil rights. He explained: 'Natural rights are those which appertain to man in right of his existence. Of this kind are all the intellectual rights, or rights of the mind, and also all those rights of acting as an individual for his own comfort and happiness, which are not injurious to the natural rights of others.'[11] He distinguished between three forms of government: clerical government founded on superstition, conquerors' government founded on force, and government founded on common interest, which he called government of reason.

Before going to France, Paine had taken an active part in the American Revolution with various writings, particularly his essay *Common Sense* (1776), in which, even though a British subject, he bitterly attacked royal authority and asserted the right of the American states to their independence, using the argument so typical of genuine liberalism that the time had come to emancipate society from political power, because while society is a blessing, government, like the clothes which cover our nakedness, is the symbol of our lost innocence.[12]

Through his actions and his works, Paine represented the continuity between the two revolutions. He had no doubts that one was a development from the other, and that the American Revolution had opened the door to the revolutions in Europe: the guiding principles were identical, as was their foundation in natural law. They shared the same objective: government founded on a social contract, a republic as government which permanently rejects hereditary law, and democracy as government for all.

The relationship between the two revolutions, which was much more complex, has been continuously reviewed and debated over the last two centuries. There are two questions: what was the influence of the first revolution on the second and how decisive was it? and which revolution taken on its own was either politically or ethically superior to the other?

As far as the first question is concerned, the debate became particularly intense at the end of last century when Jellinek's famous work negated the originality of the French Declaration, raising animated responses from those who claimed the similarity was due to a common source of inspiration, and that the members of the Constituent Assembly had little knowledge of the various American Bills of Rights.[13] On close examination, however, a few differences in principle are evident: in the 1789 Declaration, 'happiness' does not appear as one of the goals to be achieved (the expression 'happiness of everyone' only appears in the Preamble), and thus 'happiness' is not the key-word which it was in various American charters, such as the Virginian one in 1776, which was known to the French and stated that some *inherent* rights were protected because they permitted the pursuit of 'happiness' and 'security'. The *philosophes* debated the questions of what constituted 'happiness' and what was the relationship between happiness and the public good, but as the liberal constitutional state gradually began to take shape, so the idea that it was the task of the state to provide for the happiness of its subjects was completely abandoned. On this point too, it was Kant who made the clearest and most illuminating statement. In defence of the genuine liberal state whose purpose was to allow the liberty of each person to be expressed on the basis of the universal law of reason, he rejected the eudomonist state which sets itself the task of making its subjects happy, and claimed instead that its only task is to give them the freedom to pursue their own happiness in the manner they see fit.[14]

Secondly, the French declaration was more intransigently individualistic that the American one. As we shall be returning to this point later, there is no need to emphasize here that the concept of society on which the two declarations were based, came to be called individualistic in the following century, almost always with a negative connotation. This concept that the isolated individual, independent from everyone else, although along with everyone else, but each one to himself, was contrary to the idea passed down over centuries that man was a political animal, and thus a social animal from the very beginning. The state of nature existing before society as formulated from Hobbes to Rousseau, the artificial creation of *homo oeconomicus* by early economists, and the Christian idea of the individual as a moral person, who has value in himself, as one of God's creatures, all combined to create this concept of the individual. Both declarations took individual man as their starting point, and the rights that they proclaimed belonged to individuals taken one by one, because they held the rights before entering any form of society. But while the common good was invoked in the French document purely in order to justify any 'social distinctions', the American charters almost always refer directly to the purpose of political association which was the 'common benefit' (Virginia), the 'good of the whole' (Maryland) and the 'common good' (Massachusetts). The members of the American constituent assemblies linked the rights of the individual to the common good of society, while the members of the French Constituent Assembly exclusively asserted the rights of the individual above all else. The Jacobin Constitution was to be inspired by a very different idea which stands out in Article I: 'The purpose of society is the common happiness', and prioritizes everything which concerns the whole over everything which concerns the individual, the common good over the rights of the constituent parts.

As for the question of which was ethically and politically superior, the controversy goes way back. Even during the discussion in the National Assembly, Pierre Victor Malouet, the member for Lower Alvergne and chief finance officer, expressed his disagreement with the proclamation of rights, arguing that it had worked for the Americans who 'had taken man in the heart of nature and presented him to the universe in his primitive sovereignty', and were therefore 'prepared to accept liberty in all its vigour', but it would not work equally well for the French, an 'immense multitude' of whom had no property and therefore expected the government to give them not so much liberty as security in their employment, which in any case made them dependent.[15]

Of the many accounts of this controversy, I'll choose the one which should be most familiar to the Italian public, even though I have the impression that it has been completely forgotten. In his essay *La rivoluzione francese del 1789 e la rivoluzione italiana del 1859*, Alessandro Manzoni compares the American Revolution and the French Revolution precisely through a comparison of the American Constitution of 1787 and the Declaration of 1789, and he does not hesitate to show his preference for the former, using arguments resembling those of the French financial officer. He observed that apart from the fact that the American Constitution of 1787 did not involve any prior declaration, the declarations of the preceding congresses only concerned 'a few positive and special rights of the colonies in relation to the English government and Parliament, and thus they restricted themselves to proclaiming and demanding those rights which that government had violated and that Parliament had attempted to invalidate, against an ancient and peaceful title.'[16] He concluded that the supposed similarity between the two declarations and the manner in which they were proclaimed was purely superficial, so while the American charters had their desired effect, all that could be said about the declaration by the Constituent Assembly of 1789 was that it was shortly followed by 'a time in which the contempt and breach of all rights reached such a point as to make it questionable whether there is any historical parallel at all.'[17]

Let us leave the dispute over the relationship between the two declarations to the historians. Although the revolution of the thirteen colonies had an immediate impact in Europe and the American myth was rapidly formed in the old continent, it was the French Revolution which for about two centuries constituted the ideal model for those who fought for their own emancipation and the liberation of their people. The principles of 1789 constituted, whether we like it or not, an obligatory reference point for the friends and foes of liberty, invoked by the former and abominated by the latter. On the immediate, subterranean and expansive force of the French Revolution in Europe, let me remind you of Heine's splendid imagery, which compared the excitement of the Germans on hearing the news of what was happening in France to the murmur issuing, even far from the sea, from the large shells which are used to ornament mantelpieces: 'When in Paris the waves of the revolution rose, seethed and raged stormily on the great human ocean, German hearts murmured and grew excited on the other side of the Rhine.'[18]

The inspiration of the principles of 1789 have echoed through many crucial moments in our history. I shall limit myself to two of them: the Risorgimento and the opposition to fascism. While predicting a new era which he called 'social', Mazzini acknowledged that the Declaration of 1789 summarized the 'results of the Christian era, confirming beyond doubt and raising to a political dogma, the liberties attained in the domain of the Idea by the Graeco-Roman world, the equality attained by the Christian world and the brotherhood which is the immediate consequence of these two terms'.[19] Carlo Rosselli, in *Socialismo liberale*, a book stating his political programme, written in internal exile and published in France in 1930, argued that the principle of liberty which spread to cultural life during the seventeenth century, reached its high point with the Encyclopaedia and 'finally triumphed in the political sphere with the Revolution of 1789 and its Declaration of Rights'.[20]

I did say whether we like it or not.[21] The condemnation of the principles of 1789 has been a recurring theme of every anti-revolutionary movement, a starting with De Maistre and continuing right up to Action Française. Suffice it to quote that prince of reactionary writers Friedrich Nietzsche (who for some time has become the darling of the new left which has lost its bearings), who wrote in one of his last fragments published postumously: 'Our hostility to the Revolution does not concern its cruel stage or the immorality which it involved, but rather its crowd mentality, the truths by which it still operates and its infectious image of "justice and liberty", which ensnares all mediocre souls, and encourages the overthrow of the authority of the upper classes.'[22] He was shortly to be echoed by his perhaps unknowing Italian disciples, who derided 'apotheosis of the high-flown bombast of the French Revolution: Justice, Fraternity, Equality and Liberty'.[23]

The doctrinal nucleus of the Declaration is contained in the first three articles: the first concerns the natural condition of individuals which precedes the formation of civil society, the second concerns the purpose of political society which comes, if not chronologically, at least axiologically after the state of nature, the third concerns the principle of the legitimacy of power which is due the nation.

The formula of the first article: 'Men are born and remain free and equal in rights' has been repeated almost literally in Article I of the Universal Declaration of Human Rights: 'All human beings are born free and equal in dignity and rights'. Rousseau had written at the beginning of *The Social Contract*: 'Man is born free and everywhere in chains'. As has been said many times, this was an ideal and not a natural birth. The current doctrine was that men were born neither free nor equal. The belief in a mythical golden age went back to ancient times and was reaffirmed during the

Renaissance, but it was replaced by the theory of man's savage origins and primitive barbarity, which went from Lucretius to Vico. The idea that men were born free and equal in the state of nature described by Locke was a rational hypothesis: it was not a factual statement or historical truth. It was a rational need and the only means to reverse radically the centuries-old concept of political power as power over men, the *imperium*, which proceeds from the top downwards. This theory was to be used, according to Locke, 'to understand political power aright, and derive it from its original'.[24] This was precisely the purpose which the Constituent Assembly set itself when immediately after Article 2 it declared: 'the aim of every political association is the preservation of the natural and indefeasible rights of man', which are liberty, property, security and resistance to oppression. The article does not use the term 'social contract', but the idea of a contract is implicit in the word 'association'. 'Association' here can only mean a society based on a contract. The two articles are linked by the fact that the first refers to equality in rights and the second specifies what these rights are, while equality does not appear among them. It does, however, reappear in Article 6 which provides for equality before the law, and in Article 13 which provides for fiscal equality.

Of the four rights listed, only liberty is defined (Article 4), and it is defined as the right 'to be able to do anything which does not harm others' which was different to current definition found in Hobbes and Montesquieu, which stated that liberty was the ability to do everything permitted by the laws, and to Kant's definition that my liberty extends for as much as it is compatible with the liberty of others. Security was to be defined in Article 8 of the 1793 Constitution as the 'protection afforded by society to each of its members for preservation of their person, rights and property'.

Property, which the final article of the Declaration considers 'a sacred and inviolable right', was to attract the criticism of socialists and led to the 1789 Revolution being consigned to history as a bourgeois revolution. Its inclusion among the natural rights went back to an ancient legal tradition which thus long preceded the affirmation of the doctrines of natural law. It was a consequence of the independence in classical Roman Law of private law from public law, the doctrine of the original methods of acquiring property through one's own labour, and subsequent methods through deeds and succession, both of which occur entirely within the private sphere. In more recent times, Locke's well-known theory, as one of the principal inspirators of modern liberty, was that property derives from one's own labours, which is an activity which occurred before the state and occurs outside it. Contrary to what one might think today after the historic demands of the propertyless against the propertied classes under the leadership of the nineteenth-century socialist movements, the right to property was for centuries considered a bulwark, the most powerful bulwark, against the arbitrary power of the monarch. It was that most rigorous theoretician of the absolutism, Thomas Hobbes, who had the boldness to claim that the theory 'that every private man has an absolute Propriety in his Goods, such as excludeth the Right of the Soveraign' was sedition, and therefore to be condemned in a state based on the principles of reason.[25]

It is incontrovertible that Locke's thought was also behind the affirmation of the right to resist oppression, although the idea was much more ancient. Having argued that the reason man enters society is the preservation of his property as well as his liberty, Locke then deduced that when the government violates these rights, it puts itself in a state of war against its own people who from that moment are released from all ties of obedience, and there is nothing else but 'the common refuge which God hath provided all men against force and violence',[26] in other words to recover one's original liberty and resist. In legal terms, the right to resist is a secondary right in the same way as secondary norms provide for the protection of primary norms: it is a secondary right which is triggered at a secondary stage when the primary rights of liberty, property and security have been trampled on. The right to resist is also different in that it is triggered to protect the other rights, but cannot itself be protected, and therefore is exercised at one's own risk. To be strictly logical, no government can guarantee the exercise of the right to resist, which occurs precisely when the citizen no longer acknowledges the government's authority, and the government in turn has no further obligation to the citizen. Kant was possibly referring to this article when he said that 'in order for the people to be authorized to resist, there should be a public law which permits it',[27] but such a provision would be contradictory, because from the moment in which the sovereign allows resistance against himself, he ceases to be sovereign and the subject becomes sovereign in his place. It is impossible that the members of the constituent assembly did not realize the contradiction. But, as George Lefèbvre explained, the inclusion of the right to resistance among the natural rights was due to the recent memory of 14 July and the fear of another assault by the aristocracy, and was therefore nothing more than a posthumous justification of the struggle against the *ancien régime*.[28] The right to resistance does not appear in the 1948 Universal Declaration of Human Rights, but the Preamble states that the human rights, which are to be listed, must be protected 'if one wishes to avoid that people as a last resort are forced to rebel against tyranny and oppression'. Which is to say that resistance is not a right but in certain conditions a necessity (as shown by the word 'forced').

The third article according to which 'the principle of all sovereignty resides essentially in the nation', faithfully reflects the debate which had taken place in June and the rejection of Count Mirabeau's proposal to adopt the word 'people', which differentiated from the other two classes, in favour of 'nation' which was more comprehensive, unifying and all-inclusive, proposed by Abbot Sieyès, and which gave rise to the name National Assembly. 'Nation' expressed the concept which was destined to become one of the cornerstones of every future democratic government, in that it cannot be divided into classes or estates which once divided society, and in its unity and indivisibility is composed not of separate bodies but single individuals, each taken on his own, in accordance with the principle which from then on justified the diffidence of every democratic government for the representation of interest groups.[29] The concept of the united and indivisible sovereignty of the nation also implies the rejection of the rigid mandates. This rejection, which was firmly argued for by Sieyès, was suggested in Article 6 according to which the law is an expression of the general will, and explicitly formulated in Article 8 of the Preamble to the Law of 22 December 1789 which states: 'The representatives nominated by the National Assembly by the Departments must be considered representatives not of a particular department, but as representatives of all the departments together, that is of the entire nation'. Individual representation and the rejection of rigid mandates were the two institutions which together destroyed the society based on estates, where each estate had its own separate legal status and individuals were not equal either in terms of rights or before the law. From this point of view, the Declaration can truly be said to be the official demise of the *ancien régime*,[30] although the *coup de grâce* was not given until the Preamble to the 1791 Constitution which bluntly stated that 'there is no more nobility, nor peerage, nor hereditary distinction, nor distinction of order or feudal regime. There is for no part of the nation and for no individual, any privilege or exception to the law common to all the French.'[31]

The Declaration, since its proclamation right up to the present day, has provoked two recurring but opposite criticisms: it has been accused of excessive abstraction generally by reactionaries and conservatives, and of excessive links with the interests of one particular class by Marx and the left in general.

The accusation of abstraction has been repeated an infinite number of times, and besides, anti-Enlightenment currents of thought constantly dwell on the abstraction of Enlightenment thought. I need hardly repeat the famous quip by De Maistre who had seen Englishmen, Germans and Frenchmen, and, thanks to Montesquieu, knew about Persians, but had never seen man – that is, man in general, and was not aware of his existence. One could quote the less known but no less drastic opinion of Taine according to whom the articles of the Declaration

> were nothing but abstract dogmas, metaphysical definitions, and more or less literary axioms, and therefore more or less false, sometimes vague, sometimes contradictory, susceptible to various interpretations and opposite interpretations . . . a kind of pompous sign-board, useless and heavy which . . . is in danger of falling on the passers-by and is every day shaken by violent hands.[32]

Anyone who is not happy with these examples – one does not know whether to call them deprecations or imprecations – and wants a philosophical criticism, can read the supplement to § 539 in Hegel's *Encyclopaedia* where, among other important considerations, it states that liberty and equality have such little basis in nature that they can only be 'a product and result of the historical conscience', and in any case differ from one nation to another.[33]

But can it really be argued that the members of the French Constituent Assembly were so lacking in shrewdness, that their heads were in the clouds and their feet so far off the ground? In response to this question, it has been observed that those seemingly abstract rights were in fact intended by the Constituent Assembly to be instruments of political polemic, and each one had to be interpreted as the antithesis of the abuse of power which it wanted to combat, given that the revolutionaries, as Mirabeau said, had wished not to make an abstract declaration of rights, but an act of war against tyrants.[34] If then these rights were proclaimed as though they were inscribed on tablets of stone, outside time and history, this was due to the fact that the French Revolution, as Tocqueville explained, was a political revolution which acted like a religious revolution, which considers man in himself, without reference to the laws, customs and traditions of a people. It grafted uncommon features on to that common stock, and it had acted like a religious revolution because 'it seemed more interested in the regeneration of humankind than in the reform of France'.[35] According to Tocqueville, this was the reason that it could invoke passions which up till then even the most violent of political revolutions had not been able to produce.

The opposite criticism was that the Declaration, rather than being too abstract, was so concrete and historically determined that in reality it was not the defence of man in general, which existed without the knowledge of the author of the *St. Petersburg Evenings*, but of the bourgeoisie, which existed in flesh and blood, and championed the emancipation of their class against the aristocracy, without too much concern for the rights of what was to be called the fourth estate. This position was developed by the young Marx in 'The Jewish Question', too well known for us to examine yet again, and ritually repeated by successive generations of Marxists. No longer the abstract and universal man! The man referred to in the Declaration was in reality bourgeois, the rights defended by the Declaration were bourgeois rights, the rights of egotistical man, as Marx explained, of man separated from other men and from the community, of man 'as a self-sufficient monad.'[36]

This interpretation mistook the historical situation in which the demand for these rights was born, which was undoubtedly the struggle of the third estate against the aristocracy, for a question of principle, and could only see the citizen in the man, and the bourgeois in the citizen. I consider the consequences of this misinterpretation of a factual question to have been disastrous, but I also think that with the benefit of hindsight we can understand this better than our fathers did. But we are still too enclosed within this historical current to be able to understand exactly how it will end up. I find it difficult to see how one can deny that the affirmation of human rights, starting from the libertarian ones or rather the rights of individual liberty, is one of the mainstays of universal political thought which we cannot go back on.

Marx's accusation against the Declaration was that it was inspired by an individualistic concept of society. The accusation is accurate, but is it acceptable?

It is certainly true that the Declaration's approach to the eternal question of the relationship between rulers and the ruled is that of the individual, perceived as the holder of sovereign power, because in the hypothetical state of nature existing before society, he had no power above him. Political power, or the power of associated individuals, came later. It is power which is born from a convention, a product of human invention, like a machine. Indeed according to Hobbes, whose rational examination of the state starts with the rigorous consideration of individuals, the state can be defined as the most ingenious and beneficial of machines, the *machina machinarum*. This point of view represents a radical inversion of the traditional classical and medieval view of political thought, in which the two prevailing metaphors for power are the shepherd (the people being the flock) and the helmsman or *gubernator* (the people being the crew). The modern state was born from this inversion, first as the liberal state in which the individuals who claimed sovereign power are only a part of society, then democratic in which they are potentially everyone, and finally social, in which individuals who have all become sovereign without class distinction claim social as well as libertarian rights, and these too are individual rights: the citizens' state where citizens are no longer just the middle class or the citizens which Aristotle defined at the beginning of book three of the *Politics* as those who can accede to public office and who are still a minority in a democracy even after discounting slaves and foreigners.[37]

The traditional attitude was to attribute the individual not with rights but mainly with duties, starting with the duty to obey the laws, which were the commands of the sovereign. Moral and legal codes over the centuries from the Ten Commandments to the Laws of the Twelve Tables have been sets of imperative rules which establish individual obligations not rights. Let us take another look at the first two articles. First there is the statement that individuals have rights; next there is the statement that government, as a direct consequence of these rights, undertakes to guarantee them. The traditional relationship between the rights of rulers and the duties of subjects is inverted. Even in the so-called charters of rights which preceded the American ones in 1776 and the French one in 1789, from the Magna Charta to the 1689 Bill of Rights, rights and liberties were never recognized as existing prior to the power of the sovereign, but were granted or agreed, and had to appear as unilateral acts by the sovereign, even if they were in fact a pact between the subjects and the sovereign. This meant that without concessions by the sovereign the subject had no rights at all.[38] The same was to occur in the nineteenth century, when it was claimed that the emerging constitutional monarchies were granted by the sovereigns: the fact that these constitutions were the consequence of a conflict between the king and his subjects which was concluded with a pact was not allowed to erase the sacred image of power, whereby whatever the citizens obtain is as a result of the gracious munificence of the monarch.

The declarations of rights were destined to upset this image, and gradually this is what they did. Today the very concept of democracy is inseparable from the concept of human rights. If you eliminate the individualistic concept of society, you will no longer be able to justify democracy as a form of government. What better way to define democracy than as a state in which individuals, that is all individuals, have their share of sovereignty? How else could we have irreversibly consolidated this concept, if not by inverting the relationship between power and liberty, by putting liberty before power? I have often said that when we refer to democracy, it would be more correct to speak of the sovereignty of citizens, rather than sovereignty of the people. 'People' is an ambiguous term, which has been used by all the modern dictatorships. It is an abstraction which can be deceiving: it is not clear what sections of the individuals living on a given territory constitute the 'people'. Collective decisions are not taken by the people, but by the individuals it is composed of, whether they are many or few. In a democracy, collective decisions are taken directly or indirectly only by single individuals in the moment in which they place their voting paper in the ballot box. This might seem disagreeable to those who cannot perceive society other than as an organism, but whether they like it or not, democratic society is not an organic body, but the sum of its individuals. If this were not the case, the majority principle would have no justification, yet it is the fundamental rule of democratic decision-making. The majority is the result of a simple arithmetical sum where what is being counted, one by one, are the votes of single individuals. The individualistic and organic conceptions of society are irreconcilable. It is absurd to ask oneself which is truer in an absolute sense. It is not absurd, but absolutely rational, to affirm that the only one which is true for understanding and explaining the nature of democracy is the former and not the latter.[39]

One should distrust those who advocate an anti-individualistic concept of society. Practically all the reactionary doctrines have argued against individualism. Burke said: 'Individuals pass like shadows; the commonwealth is fixed and stable'. De Maistre said: 'To subject government to individual discussion would be to destroy it'. Lamennais said: 'Individualism destroys the very idea of obedience and duty, thereby destroying both power and law'.[40] It would not be too difficult to find similar quotations by the anti-democratic left. On the other hand, there is not a single democratic constitution, such as the Italian Republic's, which does not presuppose the existence of single individuals who have rights precisely because that is what they are. And how could one affirm that they are 'inviolable', if one did not presuppose that, axiologically, the individual is superior to the society which he or she has come to be part of?

The individualistic concept of society has come a long way. Human rights which have been and continue to be asserted in the constitutions of single states, have today been recognized and formally proclaimed in the context of the international community, with consequences which have literally turned the doctrine and practice of international law upside down: each individual has been raised to the potential status of an active member of the international community, while up till now its active members have clearly been the sovereign states.[41] Thus the law of peoples has been transformed into the law of peoples and individuals, and alongside international law as external public law or *ius publicum europaeum*, there is emerging a new law which we could call by Kant's term 'universal civil society', even though Kant restricted it to the right of every man to be treated as a friend and not an enemy, wherever he went. Kant termed this the right to 'hospitality'. But even within these limitations, Kant perceived cosmopolitan right not as 'fantastic or exaggerated', but as one of the necessary conditions for the pursuit of perpetual peace in a historical era in which 'a violation of rights in *one* part of the world is felt *everywhere*'.[42]

As I said at the beginning, Kant viewed the enthusiasm which greeted the French Revolution as a sign of humanity's moral disposition, and it was he who placed this extraordinary event within the prophetic history of mankind – that is to say, within a history whose precise dates are not known, but whose premonitory signs we can distinguish. According to him, one of these premonitory signs was precisely the birth of a 'constitution founded on natural law', which made it possible to give a positive answer to the question: 'Is the human race continually improving?' He said that the event had had such an effect on the spirit as never to be forgotten, 'since it has revealed in human nature an aptitude and power for improvement which no politician could have thought up'.[43] Now that we have reached the end of a century which has witnessed two world wars, an era of tyrannies and the threat of annihilation through war, we can perhaps smile at the optimism of a philosopher who lived in an age in which faith in inexorable progress was almost universal. But can we seriously argue that the idea of a constitution founded on natural law has been forgotten? Isn't the question of human rights, which monarchs had to face following the 1789 Declaration, more topical than ever? Like peace and international justice, it is one of the great themes which peoples and governments are dragged towards, whether they like it or not. Just as the national declarations were the premise for the birth of the modern democracies, the Universal Declaration of Human Rights will perhaps be the premise for the democratization of the international system which is essential for ending the traditional system of balances in which peace is always a truce between two wars, and the commencement of an era of stable peace which does not have war as its alternative.

I realize that statements of this kind can only be made in the context of the prophetic history which Kant spoke of, and therefore a history whose predictions do not have the certainty of scientific forecasts (but have there ever been scientific forecasts in human history?). Unfortunately I also acknowledge that on the whole prophets of doom have not been believed, and the events they foretold have come true, while the prophets of good times have been immediately believed, and the events they foretold have not come true. Why shouldn't it be the case for just once that the prophet of doom is wrong and the prophet of good times is right?

Notes

1 G. Lefèbvre, *The Coming of the French Revolution*, trans. R.R. Palmer (Princeton: Princeton University Press, 1947), p. 174 (original title: *Quatre-vingt-neuf*). One of the most important living historians of the French Revolution, François Furet, having recognized that 'the 1789 reference-point has disappeared from French politics', admits that this is due to the fact that the debate has shifted from the past revolution to the future one, hence the French Revolution is not just the Republic but also an unrestricted promise of equality, and to restore its mystery one simply has to perceive it as a blueprint for the universal history rather than as a national institution' (*Critique of the French Revolution*)

2 A. de Tocqueville, *L'ancien régime et la révolution*, in *Œuvres complètes*, vol. II (Paris: Mayer, 1952), p. 72.

3 See entry for 'Enthousiasme' in the *Dictionnaire philosophique*, where enthusiasm is contrasted with reason because, while reason demonstrates how things actually are, enthusiasm is like wine 'qui peut exciter tant de tumultes dans les vaisseaux sanguins et de si violentes vibrations dans les

nerfs, que la raison en est tout-à-fait détruite'. But as is well known, Voltaire was preceded by Locke who dedicated a chapter to enthusiasm in his *Essay Concerning Human Understanding*, IV, 19. The history of the concept of enthusiasm would merit considerably more investigation, but it will have to suffice to refer to N. Abbagnano's entry for 'Entusiasmo' in the *Dizionario di filosofia* (Turin: UTET, 1961), which has been republished several times.

4 I. Kant, 'A Renewed Attempt to Answer the Question: "Is the Human Race Continually Improving" ' (*The Contest of Faculties*) in *Political Writings* (Cambridge: Cambridge University Press, 1991), pp. 182–3. For the complex question of the relationship between Kant and the Revolution, I refer to my work *Diritto e stato nel pensiero di Emanuele Kant* (Turin: Giappichelli, 1969), pp. 225 ff. For a detailed analysis and original interpretation of Kant's thought in relation to the French Revolution, see D. Losurdo, *Autocensura e compromesso nel pensiero politico di Kant* (Naples: Bibliopolis, 1983).

5 Kant, *For Perpetual Peace* (1795), *Political Writings*, p. 99 n. For Kant's theory, of liberty, I refer to my article 'Kant e le due libertà', in N. Bobbio, *Da Hobbes a Kant* (Naples: Morano, 1965), pp. 147–63.

6 J.-J. Rousseau, *The Social Contract*, I, 8, trans. G.D.H. Cole (London: Dent, 1973), p. 178.

7 These famous expressions can be found at the beginning of the last chapter of *Lectures on the Philosophy of World History* (Cambridge: Cambridge University Press, 1975), entitled 'The French Revolution and its Consequences'. On this question, see the celebrated, essay by J. Ritter, 'Hegel und die französische Revolution' (1956), in *Metaphysik und Politik. Studien zu Aristoteles und Hegel* (Frankfurt am Main: Suhrkamp, 1969), pp. 183–233.

8 E. Burke, *Reflections on the Revolution in France* (1790), ed. C.C. O'Brian (London: Penguin Books, 1969), p. 182. G. Tamagnini has recently produced a study of Burke, with particular reference to *Reflections*, entitled *Un giusnaturalismo ineguale. Studio su Edmund Burke* (Milan: Giuffré, 1988).

9 Burke, *Reflections*, p. 183.

10 Ibid.

11 T. Paine, *The Rights of Man*, ed. H. Collins (London: Pelican, 1969) p. 90. The transition from natural rights to civil rights is explained by Paine in these terms: as men are not capable of preserving all their natural rights when they do not have the power to do so, they renounce those rights which only the establishment of a common power will allow them to preserve. In his own words: 'The natural rights which are not retained, are all those in which, though the right is perfect in the individual, the power to execute them is defective' (p. 90). This passage clearly shows the in-

fluence of Locke, according to whom the transition from the state of nature to civil society occurred through the renunciation of some natural rights which individuals made or were forced to make. This renunciation can vary in extensiveness: very limited in Locke's model, given that the only natural right which one has to renounce on entering civil society is that of self-defence. Equally Paine, having stated that man in the state of nature has the power to judge, recognized that not having the power to impose it on his own, 'he therefore deposits this right in the common stock of society, and takes the arm of society, of which he is part, in preference and in addition to his own' (pp. 90–1).

12 At the beginning of *Common Sense* (1776), Paine keenly expressed the contrast between good society and the bad government which was to become an essential aspect of the concept of a 'minimum state': 'Society is produced by our wants, and government by our wickedness; the former promotes our happiness *positively* by uniting our affections, the latter *negatively* by restraining our vices', *Common Sense*, ed. I. Kramnick (Harmoudsworth: Penguin Books, 1976) p. 65.

13 The work concerned was *Die Erklärung der Menschen- und Bürgerrecht* (1896), which created widespread debate; see Lefèbvre, *The Coming of the French Revolution*, p. 214. In reality the American texts were fairly well known, especially through Lafayette.

14 I have chosen the following from the innumerable passages by Kant which could be quoted to demonstrate his aversion to the paternalistic state, because of its clarity and decisiveness: 'The worst kind of despotism imaginable is a government based on the principle of benevolence towards the people, like a father's government of his children, i.e. a paternalistic government (*imperium paternale*) in which the subjects, like children before the age of majority, cannot distinguish between what is good for them and what is bad, are forced to behave passively and await the decision of the head of state as how to make them happy' (*On the Common Saying: 'This May Be True in Theory, but it Does not Apply in Practice'*, in *Political Writings*, p. 74). A fundamental work on this topic is G.J. Schochet's *Partiarchalism in Political Thought* (Oxford: Oxford University Press, 1975). See also by the same author, 'Patriarchalism, Naturalism and the Rise of the Conventional State' in *Materiali per una storia della cultura giuridica*, vol. XIV, 2 (1984), pp. 223–37, which concludes: 'The disappearance of the family from Anglo-Saxon political thought more than two centuries ago is undoubtedly related to the triumph of the rigid and presumably liberal distinction between the so-called public and private, and the subsequent exclusion of the private sphere, including the family, from public debate' (p. 334). See also E. Diciotti, 'Paternalism', in

Materiali per una storia della cultura giuridica, vol. XVI, 2 (1986), pp. 557–86, who quotes R. Dworkin's definition of paternalism which echoes Kant's: 'By paternalism I mean more or less that interference with a person's freedom of action which is justified by motives entirely related to the welfare, happiness, needs, interests or values of the person subjected to the interference' (p. 560).

15 Quoted by A. Saitta, *Costituenti e costituzioni della Francia moderna* (Turin: Einaudi, 1952), p. 39.

16 A. Manzoni, *La rivoluzione francese del 1789 e la rivoluzione italiana de 1859*, in *Tutte le opere di Alessandro Manzoni* (Florence: Barbera, 1928), p. 1110. The comparison, however, is not entirely accurate because, as has been pointed out by G. Del Vecchio, *La Dichiarazione dei diritti dell'uomo e del cittadino* (1903) in *Contributi alla storia del pensiero giuridico e filosofico* (Milan: Giuffré, 1963), pp. 141–216, Manzoni only knew the text of the American Constitution and not the texts of the declarations of rights proclaimed by the American states which preceded it (p. 188). This observation was repeated a few years later by F. Ruffini, *I diritti di libertà* (Turin: Gobetti Editore, 1926), pp. 84–5, with the categoric conclusion: 'His [Manzoni's] distinction simply does not stand up'. On this question, see L. Mannori, 'Manzoni e il fenomeno rivoluzionario', *Quaderni fiorentini*, vol. XV (1986), pp. 7–106.

17 Manzoni, *La rivoluzione francese*, p. 1114.

18 The passage is taken from the work *Zur Geschichte der Religion und Philosophie in Deutschland* (1834), which I have quoted from V. Verra, *La Rivoluzione francese nel pensiero tedesco contemporaneo* (Turin: Edizioni di Filosofia, 1969), p. 3.

19 G. Mazzini, *Dell'iniziativa rivoluzionaria in Europa* (1834), in *Scritti editi e inediti* (Milan: 1863), vol. V, p. 67. This invocation was written by Mazzini as young man. As is well known, he believed that the French Revolution had justly destroyed an old and unjust society, but needed to be over-hauled by a new revolution which would have replaced the age of the individual with the age of association, and the Declaration of Rights with the Declaration of Duties.

20 C. Rosselli, *Socialismo liberale* (Turin: Einaudi, 1979), p. 90. The nucleus of the doctrine of liberal socialism consisted of the conviction that the future socialist revolution would not be the antithesis but the necessary development of the 1789 Revolution. Roselli was inspired by the ideas of one of his teachers, Rodolfo Mondolfo, who at the beginning of the century had written an essay 'Dalla Dichiarazione dei diritti al Manifesto dei comunisti', in which he demonstrated the continuity between the two texts rather than the lack of it (in *Critica sociale*, vol. XVI (1906), pp. 232–5, 329–32, 347–50).

21 While I was writing these pages, I received G. Tamagnini's book, *Rivol-uzione francese e diritto dell'uomo: alcuni pro e alcuni contro* (Modena: Macchi, 1988). The main adversaries whom the author refers to are Burke and Bentham. But unlike Burke's criticisms which were mainly political, Bentham's were essentially philosophical in that he rejected, from a position which would later be called positivist philosophy of law, that the individual could have rights which have not been granted by the state, and therefore accused the members of the French Constituent Assembly of committing a gross error. Bentham's violent diatribe against declarations of rights was contained in his *Anarchical Fallacies*, which were made known throughout Europe by E. Dumont's French translation (1816). For an examination and criticism of this text, see M.A. Cattaneo, *Il positivismo giuridico inglese* (Milan: Giuffré, 1962), pp. 150 ff.

22 F. Nietzsche, *Frammenti postumi* (1880–8), vol. VIII, ii, *Opere di Friedrich Nietzsche* (Milan: Adelphi, 1971), p. 59. This invective against the principles of 1789 reflects the whole of Nietzsche's work, with its criticism of the egalitarianism in Rousseau's thought and its contempt for democracy and socialism.

23 G. Papini and G. Prezzolini, *Vecchio e nuovo nazionalismo* (Milan: Studio Editoriale Lombardo, 1914), p. 9. For further edifying passages of this nature, I refer to my own work 'L'ideologia del fascismo' (1957), in *Il fascismo. Antologia di scritti critici*, ed. C. Casucci (Bologna: Edizioni del Mulino, 1982), pp. 598–624.

24 J. Locke, *The Second Treatise of Government*, II, 4 (Oxford: Basil Blackwell, 1946), p. 4.

25 T. Hobbes, *Leviathan*, ed. R. Tuck (Cambridge: Cambridge University Press, 1991), XXVIII, p. 224. It should be emphasized that the defence of property as a natural individual right was principally aimed against feudal property, which was condemned on the night of 4 August, the same day in which the proposal for the Declaration was approved. For the relationship between the affirmation of bourgeois property and the condemnation of feudal property, see G. Solari, *Individualismo e diritto privato* (Turin: Giappichelli, 1959 [1911]), p. 141.

26 J. Locke, *The Second Treatise on Civil Government*, p. 108.

27 I. Kant, *The Doctrine of Law*, II, *Public Law* (1786).

28 Lefèbvre, *The Coming of the French Revolution*, p. 179.

29 For a more thorough account of these debates, see P. Violante, *Lo spazio della rappresentanza*, vol. I, *Francia* (1788–9) (Palermo: Ila Palma, 1981).

30 Lefèbvre, *The Coming of the French Revolution*, p. 174.

31 For the various types of hierarchical society, see R. Mousnier, *Social Hierarchies from 1450 to the Present Day* (London: Croom Helm, 1973).

32 H.A. Taine, *Les Orgines de la France contemporaine. La Révolution, l'anarchie*. Quoted by G. Del Vecchio in *La Dichiarazione dei diritti*, p. 180. Del Vecchio's study, which is still a useful reference work contains a lengthy review of judgements on the Declaration.

33 Hegel wrote that if these two categories of liberty and equality are maintained in abstract form, as when they are perceived as natural rights existing before the state, then they 'prevent or destroy concreteness, i.e. the organization of the state, a constitution or a government in general'. It should be noted that these statements appear in a supplement to the paragraph in which Hegel defines the state as the 'organized totality' and the constitution as the 'organization of state power'. One cannot fail to notice that this is clearly an anti-individualistic concept of the state, and therefore one which rejects the social contract, a question I discuss in more detail in 'La costituzione di Hegel', in *Studi hegeliani* (Turin: Einaudi, 1981), pp. 69–83.

34 This criticism of the criticism of abstraction has already been made by P. Janet in the Introduction to the third edition of his famous *Histoire de la science politique dans ses rapports avec la morale* (Paris: n. pub., 1887), entitled *Les Déclarations des droits en Amérique et en France*, and has been taken up on several occasions. One example is G. De Ruggiero, *Storia del liberalismo europeo* (Bari: Laterza, n.d.): 'The tone of the Declaration is apparently abstract, but whoever examines the individual liberties listed with a historian's eye, soon realizes that each one represents a polemical antithesis of a specific aspect of society and the state at that time' (p. 72).

35 A. de Tocqueville, *L'ancien régime et la révolution*, p. 89. This statement by Tocqueville seems to reflect Paine's praise of the Revolution when he wrote that with the French Revolution a 'completely new and unequalled' event had occurred in the world, such that the name of revolution seemed to diminish it, as it merited the name of 'regeneration of mankind'.

36 K. Marx, 'The Jewish Question', in *Early Texts*, ed. and trans. D. McLellan (Oxford: Basil Blackwell, 1971), p. 103. The criticism of the individualism in the Declaration, using individualism in a negative sense, was not exclusive to Marx, but was commonplace in left-wing historiography (and from an opposite point of view, but with the same result, in that of the extreme right). In *La Gauche et la révolution au milieau du XIXe siècle* (Paris: Hachette, 1986), Furet recalls that for Buchez (the author of a *Histoire de la Révolution française*, 1834–48) human rights were the great mistake of the Revolution given the inappropriateness of these principals in the construction of a community, because they concern individuals defined within their own particular spheres (pp. 16 and 19).

37 Aristotle, *Politics*, 1275a (Harmondsworth: Penguin, 1981), pp. 168–71.

38 For a fuller anthology of charters of rights before and after the French Revolution, see *Derecho positivo de los derechos humanos*, ed. G. Peces-Barba, director of the Instituto de derechos humanos di Madrid (Madrid: Editorial Debate, 1987).

39 I have discussed this topic in greater detail in 'La democrazia dei moderni paragonata a quella degli antichi (e a quella dei posteri)', in *Teoria politica*, vol. III, no. 3, pp. 3–17.

40 I have taken these quotations from S. Lukes, *Individualism* (Oxford: Blackwell, 1985), pp. 3–5. This book is a useful collection of material for anyone who wants general information on the question of individualism, which classifies it into its political, economic, religious, ethical and other aspects, and contrasts it with holism.

41 For the question of human rights from the internationalist point of view, see A. Cassese, *I diritti umani nel mondo contemporaneo* (Bari: Laterza, 1988).

42 I. Kant, *For Perpetual Peace*, in *Political Writings*, pp. 107–8. See M. Sena, *Etica e cosmopolitismo in Kant* (Naples: Edizioni Parallelo 38, 1976) which draws attention to a passage in Kant's *Pragmatic View of Anthropology*, in which universal civil society is considered the supreme principle governing mankind. Kant's fundamental text on this argument is *Idea for a Universal History with a Cosmopolitan Purpose* (1784), in *Political Writings*, pp. 41–53. See also D. Archibugi, 'Le utopie della pace perpetua', *Lettera internazionale*, vol. V, no. 22, (autumn 1989), pp. 55–60, which emphasizes the novelty of Kant's 'cosmopolitan right'.

43 I. Kant, 'A Renewed Attempt to Answer the Question: "Is the Human Race Continually Improving?" ' (*The Contest of Faculties*) in *Political Writings*, p. 184.

7 The Legacy of the Great Revolution

The French Revolution instilled the powerful idea in the human imagination of an extraordinary political event which broke with historical continuity, marked the end of one era and the beginning of another. Two dates, which were very close together, can be used to symbolize these two moments: on 4 August 1789 the nobility's renunciation of their privileges marked the end of the feudal regime, and on 26 August, the approval of the Declaration of the Rights of Man marked the beginning of the new era. It hardly needs saying that the symbol is not the same thing as the reality of the facts investigated by increasingly meticulous historians. But as far as the subject of this essay is concerned, the power of the symbol has not been lessened over the years.

In fact, the declaration of 26 August had been preceded some years before by the declarations of rights or *Bills of rights* proclaimed by some American colonies in their struggle against the mother country. Comparison between the two revolutions and the respective declarations of fundamental rights is a ritual topic, which involves both a factual assessment of the relationship between the two events and a value judgement on the moral and political superiority of one or the other. The intricate arguments on the affinities and differences between the two revolutions often appear to be mere academic exercises, and the disputes over the superiority of one or the other are too ideological to be taken very seriously. There is little point in comparing a war of independence (a war of liberation, we would say today) by a people who intend to found a political constitution built in the image and likeness of the mother country (as we all know, the presidential republic was modelled on the constitutional monarchy), with the tearing down of a political regime and a social structure in order to replace them with something completely different both in terms of the relationship between the rulers and the ruled, and in terms of class domination. On the other hand, it is more reasonable or less arbitrary to compare the declarations, as long as this comparison is no longer approached in the stark terms of the clash which took place at the end of the last century between the great jurist Georg Jellinek, who stubbornly claimed that the French declaration derived from the American ones, and Emile Boutmy who equally stubbornly claimed the opposite, arguing among other things that the members of the French Constituent Assembly had little knowledge of the precedents on the other side of the ocean, an assertion which has been disproved.

The author of a lengthy article 'Droits de l'homme' which recently appeared in *Dictionnaire critique de la Révolution française*, has argued once again that 'the American example played a decisive role in the formation of the French declaration'. But first one must make a distinction between the content of a declaration and the idea itself of a declaration to precede a constitution. One can argue over the content, but the influence of the American declaration on the idea is indisputable. It was Lafayette, the hero of American independence, who was the first to present the plan for a declaration, with a text formulated 'under the eyes and with the advice' of Jefferson who was then the United States ambassador in Paris. The members of the Constituent Assembly not only knew the American model but, as Gouchet observed, their position on the planned declaration reflected their attitude to previous declarations. Pierre Victor Malouet, a monarchist and chief finance officer for Lower Auvergne, opposed the declaration by arguing that, while a new people like the Americans were 'prepared to accept liberty in all its vigour', a people like the French, composed of an immense multitude of subjects without property, expected the government to furnish 'security of employment which makes them dependent, rather than liberty'.

As far as the content of the two texts is concerned, one has to acknowledge their common origin in the tradition of natural law, which is much more decisive even in the French declaration than the influence of Rousseau, in spite of the differences that have been noted on several occasions. The most conspicuous difference is the reference in the French Declaration to the 'general will' as the holder of legislative power (Art. 6) which clearly derives from the author of *The Social Contract*. The common starting point is the assertion that man has natural rights which, being natural, preceded the establishment of civil power, and must therefore be recognized, complied with and defended. Article 2 defines them as 'indefeasible', meaning that they are never lost even by peoples who have not exercised them for long periods of time, *ab immemorabili*, unlike rights which have emerged historically and are recognized by civil laws. As soon as the news of the Parisian upheavals reached England, Edmund Burke, the first harsh critic of the French Revolution, was to put forward the famous theory of historical prescription, according to which the rights of the English received their vigour not from their being natural but from having been established through a long tradition of liberty unknown to the majority of other peoples. In contrast to the theory of historical prescription, the theory of indefeasibility is intentionally revolutionary.

In general, the assertion that man by his very nature, outside and before the formation of any social groupings, had original rights represents a real turning-point in both the theory and practice of politics, which warrants a brief description.

The political relationship, or rather the relationship between rulers and the ruled, the dominant and the dominated, the prince and the people, the sovereign and the subjects and the state and the citizens, is a power relationship which can take on three directions according to whether it is a reciprocal power relationship, the power of the former categories over the latter or the latter over the former. Traditionally, in both classical and medieval political thought, the political relationship has been considered an unequal relationship in which one category is above the other: the ruler above the ruled, the dominant above the dominated, the prince above the people, the sovereign above the subjects, and the state above the citizens. In political terminology, *potestas* comes before *libertas*, in the sense that the area of liberty reserved for the individual had to be graciously conceded by the holders of power. In Hobbesian terms, *lex* understood as the sovereign's command, comes before *jus* in the sense that *jus* or law for individuals coincides purely and simply with the *silentium legis*. The traditional legal doctrine was that public law could regulate private law, but private law could not contravene public law.

The portrayal of political power through metaphors sheds much light on this point of view. If the ruler is the shepherd (remember the dispute between Socrates and Thrasymachus on this subject), the ruled are the flock (the distinction between the moral code of the aristocracy and the moral code of the herd continued right up to Nietzsche). If the ruler is the helmsman or *gubernator*, the people are the crew who must obey; should they refuse to obey, and should they rebel and believe that they can do without the expert guidance of the commander, as in a famous passage from Plato's *Republic*, then the ship will inevitably sink. If the ruler is the father (the portrayal of the state as a great family with the sovereign as father of his people is common to all political literature, both ancient and modern), the subjects are like children who must obey their father's commands, because they have not yet reached the age of reason and cannot take responsibility for their own actions. Of the three metaphors, the last one has proved the most durable. One should recall Locke's pointed criticism of Filmer's *Patriarcha*, which claimed the power to govern descended directly from the ancient patriarchs, and Kant's farsighted criticism of all forms of paternalistic state which consider subjects to be eternal minors who have to be guided regardless of their will towards a healthy, prosperous, good and happy life. But then Locke and Kant believed in natural law or, in other words, they were both thinkers who had inverted the perspective, and carried out that 'Copernican revolution', to use one of Kant's own expressions, albeit in a different context to the one in which he used it. They no longer considered political relations *ex parte principis*, but *ex parte civium*.

In order to bring about this inversion in viewpoint which was the source of modern political thought, they needed to abandon the traditional theory which I have defined elsewhere as the

Aristotelian model, a model which perceived man as a political animal who is born within a social group, the family, and improves his own nature within a larger and inherently self-sufficient social grouping called the *polis*. They also needed to consider the individual on his own, free from all social ties and, more to the point, all political ties, in a state like the state of nature, although this was a rational hypothesis which intentionally ignored the historic origins of human societies. In the state of nature, no political power would have yet been constituted above the individual, and there would have been no positive laws to impose this or that action, thus creating a state of perfect, if hypothetical, liberty and equality. They needed to assume the existence of a state preceding every organized form of society, an original state, which precisely because it was the origin, had to be considered the birthplace and foundation of civil society. This meant that civil society was no longer a natural state like the family or other social groupings, but something artificial and intentionally built on the voluntary union of natural individuals.

To summarize then, individuals were not born free or equal as long as they were considered to have originally been members of a natural social group, such as the family, which was organized hierarchically. They were not free because they were subject to paternal authority, and they were not equal because the relationship between a father and his children is a relationship between superior and inferior. It was only through the hypothesis of an original state of nature without society or state, in which men lived without laws other than the natural laws that are not imposed by an external authority, but are obeyed by the conscience, that one can argue the audacious, contrived and patently anti-historical principle that men are born free and equal. One can find this principle at the start of the Declaration which solemnly states: 'Men are born and remain free and equal in rights', words which were to be repeated to the letter, a century and a half later, in Article I of the Universal Declaration of Human Rights: 'All men are born free and equal in dignity and rights'. In reality men are born neither free nor equal. Reason demands that men should be born free and equal, but it is not a statement of fact, nor is it a historical reality. It is a hypothesis that permits the radical inversion of the traditional concept that the power over men, called *imperium*, proceeds from the top down. According to Locke himself, this hypothesis was to be used 'to understand political power well, and to derive it from its origin'. This was clearly an ideal and not a historical origin.

Any portrayal of how this inversion of viewpoint was arrived at, probably has to be rather speculative. It would be nothing less than a description of the birth of the individualistic concept of society and history, which is the radical antithesis of the organic concept, as the organic concept held that the whole (society) preceded the parts, to quote a statement by Aristotle which was to be quoted by Hegel. By inverting the relationship between the whole and the parts, the individualistic concept of society and history claimed that the individual came first and society came afterwards. Society is for the individual, and not the individual for society. Even this principle is formally stated in Article 2 of the Declaration, where it lists the four natural rights which man originally possessed, and asserted that 'the purpose of every political association is the preservation' of these rights. The purpose of political organization for the organic concept of society is the preservation of the whole. It has no room for rights which claim not only to precede it but even to transcend it, or indeed to submit it to their own requirements. The very expression 'political association' is completely alien to the organic concept: 'association' refers to a voluntary social formation, based on an agreement. Even though the expression 'social contract' does not appear in the Declaration, the word 'association' presupposes it. The parts are a function of the whole in an organic concept of society; the whole is the result of the free will of the parts in an individualistic concept.

One cannot place too much emphasis on the historical importance of this inversion. The modern democracy (democracy in the modern sense of the word) which was born from the individualistic concept of society, should properly be defined not as the ancients defined it, 'power of the people', but as power of individuals taken one by one, of all the individuals who make up society, sustained by a few essential rules. One of these fundamental rules grants every person equally with the right to participate freely in the collective decision-making which binds the whole community.

A modern democracy rests on the sovereignty not of the people but of its citizens. The people are an abstraction which has often been used to cover very different realities. It has been said that after Nazism the word *Volk* became impossible to articulate, and we can all remember that the official newspaper of the fascist regime was called *Il popolo d'Italia*. I do not wish to be misunderstood, but even the word *peuple* became suspect after the way it was abused during the French Revolution: the people of Paris overthrew the Bastille, carried out the September massacres, judged and executed the king. But what has this people to do with the citizens of a contemporary democracy? The same ambiguity was hidden in the concept of *populus romanus* or the people of a medieval city, which also made the distinction between *popolo grasso and popolo minuto*.* As true democracy gradually established itself, the word 'people' became increasingly empty and rhetorical, although the Italian constitution does proclaim that 'sovereignty belongs to the people'. In a modern democracy, collective decisions are always taken solely by the citizens as individuals, when they place their voting paper in the ballot box. It is not a collective body. If this were not the case, there would be no justification for majority rule, which is the fundamental rule of democratic government. The majority is the result of an arithmetical sum which quantifies the votes of single individuals, precisely those individuals whom the fiction of a state of nature before civil society provided with the concept of original rights, including the right to determine the laws that affect them through their own free will.

If you eliminate the individualistic concept of society, you will no longer be able to justify democracy as a good form of government. All reactionary doctrines have argued against individualism. In Burke one reads that 'Individuals pass like shadows; the commonwealth is fixed and stable'. De Maistre peremptorily declared: 'To subject government to individual discussion would be to destroy it.' Lamennais stated: 'Individualism destroys the

* *Popolo grasso* and *popolo minuto*: a distinction made in medieval Florence between the richer and poorer sections of the merchant and guild class or 'bourgeoisie', literally meaning the 'fat people' and the 'little people'. These terms expressed a certain aristocratic contempt for both [*translator's note*].

very idea of obedience and duty, thereby destroying both power and law.' In contrast, there is not a single democratic constitution which does not presuppose the existence of individual rights, and which therefore does not start with the idea that first come the rights of the individual citizen, and then comes the power of the government which the citizens constitute and control through their own liberties.

The debate in the National Assembly on the Declaration lasted for fifteen days from 11 to 26 August. Various proposals were put forward, one after another, and on 12 August, a commission of five members was set up to co-ordinate them. After three days, Mirabeau presented a draft in the name of the commission, which consisted of nineteen articles taken from twenty different proposals. On 18 August, a bitter conflict broke out. This first text was put aside and an anonymous proposal by the Assembly's Sixth Office was adopted. After other incidents which made the debate somewhat troubled and chaotic, the debate on the single articles took place from 20 to 26 August. The twenty-four articles were gradually reduced to seventeen, and the last of them, which concerned the sacred and inviolable nature of property, was approved on 26 August.

There were three preliminary problems which had to be resolved: first, whether or not it was fitting to have a declaration; second, if it was fitting, whether it should be proclaimed by itself or as a premise to the constitution, and in this case whether it should be postponed; and third, whether, once the idea of independent proclamation had been accepted, it should be accompanied by a declaration of duties, as Abbot Gregoire was demanding. The intermediate position prevailed, and it was the right decision. The Declaration, which was approved as an independent text quite separate from the future constitution, was to have its own glorious history, as everyone has to acknowledge. It entered history under the stirring title of the '1789 Principles'.

It can be clearly seen from the Preamble which introduces the articles, that the members of the Constituent Assembly were fully aware of the historical significance of what they were doing. This Preamble argues that the Declaration is necessary because 'the ignorance and contempt of human rights are the sole causes of public misadventures and the corruption of governments'. The fundamental article is the second one which expressly and categorically proclaims these rights: liberty, property, security and resistance to oppression.

The Declaration has repeatedly been the object of formal and substantial criticisms. As far as the former are concerned, it is not very difficult to find the contradictions and deficiencies. Firstly, of the four rights proclaimed, only the first, liberty, is defined, and is defined in Article 3 as 'the power to do anything that does not harm others', giving rise to the rule in the following article whereby 'the law has only the right to prohibit those actions which are harmful to society'. In Article 5, however, it is implicitly defined as the right to do anything which is not prohibited or demanded, a more classical definition, by which liberty is interpreted negatively as *silentium legis*, or the space which is left free by the lack of imperative laws, whether negative or positive. Unlike the first, this second definition is implicit, because the text limits itself to the tortuous statement that 'everything which is not prohibited by the law, cannot be impeded, and no one can be forced to do that which the law does not order'. The two definitions diverge, because the first defines an individual's liberty in relation to other individuals, and the second defines an individual's liberty in relation to state power. The first is limited by the right of others not to be harmed, and reflects the classical *principium iuris* of *neminem laedere*. The second deals exclusively with the possibility of excessive state power. In reality, the first is not so much a definition of liberty as a definition of tort, and the second is a definition of liberty, but only negative liberty. Positive liberty or liberty as autonomy is implicitly defined in Article 6, which states that as the law is an expression of the general will, 'all citizens have the right to be involved in its formation either personally or through their representatives'.

Property had no need to be defined: it is only referred to in the last article which establishes a general and absolutely obvious principle of law that property, being a sacred and inviolable right, cannot be restricted except for reasons of the public good. Security is not defined, but it was to be defined in Article 8 of the 1793 Constitution. The questions relating to security are confronted in Articles 7, 8, 9 and 10, which summarize the general principles relating to personal liberty or Habeas Corpus. Personal liberty is historically the first of the rights which subjects of a state have demanded and for which they obtained protection, going back to the Magna Charta, generally considered to be the forerunner of the bills of rights. But personal liberty must be clearly distinguished from the other natural rights: the former is the foundation for the constitutional state founded on the principle of the rule of law, the latter are the premise for the liberal or the restricted state. The former is aimed against arbitrary power, and the latter against absolute power. The fact that power tends to be more arbitrary the more it is absolute, does not mean that they both raise the same problems in terms of the means used to combat them. The gradual recognition of civil liberties, not to speak of political liberty, involves the achievement of further gains beyond the protection of personal liberty. If anything, it is the right of property which precedes the protection of personal liberty. Property has always been a more protected area than that of the person. There was no need for an article in the Declaration to proclaim property a sacred and inviolable right, even in absolutist states property has been more secure than the person. One of the most important questions for the *philosophes* was criminal law reform, that is to say, changes to the law affecting the degree of liberty enjoyed by the person.

Apart from personal liberty, the Declaration provided for religious freedom in the extremely contentious Article 9, and freedom of thought and of the press in Article 10. There are no provisions for freedom of assembly and even less so for the freedom of association, which was the last liberty to be attained and which gave rise to the pluralist society of modern democracy. Two articles concern fiscal rights and obligations. Article 16 proclaims the strange principle that a society which does not guarantee rights and does not separate powers does not have a constitution. The influence of that famous chapter in Montesquieu's *The Spirit of the Laws* on English liberty is quite evident here, but this does not change the fact that theoretically and historically it is a senseless statement. It confuses 'constitution' with 'good constitution', or rather with a constitution which was held to be good in a given historical context (but then even Aristotle called *politeia*, i.e. constitution, the best form of government).

Something still has to be said about the right to resistance which was submitted in many of the draft declarations as entirely obvious. But not so obvious, given that Article 7 states that every citizen *appelé ou saisi* on the basis of the law, must immediately obey or be deemed guilty of 'resistance'. In reality, the right to resistance is different from the other rights, always supposing that one can correctly call it a right. It is not a primary but a secondary right, whose exercise occurs only when the primary rights – that is, the rights of liberty, property and security – have been violated. The individual can make use of the right to resistance only as a last resort, as *extrema ratio*, in order to protect himself once the primary rights have failed to afford him protection. It therefore cannot itself be safeguarded and must be exercised at one's own risk. Strictly speaking, no government can guarantee the exercise of a right which is triggered precisely at the moment in which the government's authority fails, and the relationship between the state and the citizen is no longer legal but *de facto* and based on rule by the strongest. The members of the Constituent Assembly were perfectly aware of this contradiction, but as Georges Lefèbvre explains, the insertion of the right to resistance was due to the fear of another attack by the aristocrats, and therefore constituted a justification for the destruction of the *ancien régime* after the event.

The practical criticisms of natural rights are much more serious than the formal ones, and are of two types. The first category concerns their lack of meaning, emptiness or superficiality, due to their abstractness and supposed universality. Burke, the Revolution's first adversary, was quick to express one of the harshest criticisms: 'We have not been drawn and trussed, in order that we may be filled, like stuffed birds in a museum, with chaff and rags, and paltry, blurred shreds of paper about the rights of man'. A century later, Taine was to echo his sentiments: the articles in the Declaration 'are nothing but abstract dogmas, metaphysical definitions, and more or less literary axioms, and therefore more or less false, sometimes vague, sometimes contradictory, susceptible to various opposing interpretations'.

Paradoxically, the criticism which Marx and the entire tradition of theoretical Marxism directed against the Declaration was exactly the opposite. The articles which elevated some freedoms but not others to the status of natural rights, and exalted property as sacred and inviolable were not too abstract, but if anything too concrete. They were the clear ideological expression not of universal principles, but of the interests of a specific class, the bourgeoisie, which was setting about replacing the feudal class in the domination of society and the state.

Both criticisms have had little success, nor could they have. The rights may appear abstract formulations, but as Mirabeau said right at the beginning, they had in reality to be interpreted as an extremely concrete act of war against ancient abuses of power which by that time could no longer be tolerated. More than a century later, Salvemini was to echo this view:

> The first of the Declarations was certainly abstract and metaphysical, and it is extremely arguable that you can talk about the 'natural rights' of man. . . . But one should not lose sight of the spirit of the Declaration in order to criticize the letter of it in a pedantic fashion. Each of those rights . . . represented at that time the abolition of a series of intolerable abuses and corresponds to an urgent need of the nation.

Marxist criticism was also unable to comprehend the essential feature of the proclamation of rights: they expressed the demand to restrict the excessive power of the state, a demand which contained a universal value, even if at the time it was most advantageous to the bourgeoisie. One only has to read the first of the articles which concern personal liberty: 'No one can be accused, arrested or detained, except in those cases defined by the law, etc.' (this is the article which upholds civil liberties, the principle of *nulla poena sine lege* – 'no punishment without a law'). One should also reflect on what has occurred in those countries which exhibit the woeful consequences of contempt for that principle, and once its universality is challenged, both bourgeois and proletarian are affected without distinction.

Another much more radical and more serious criticism concerns the philosophical basis for the document which starts from the premise that natural rights exist. But do they? The affirmation of these rights was the direct consequence of ascendancy of natural law in philosophy for two centuries, from Grotius to Kant. However, all the main nineteenth-century philosophical currents attack the concept of natural law, albeit from different points of view and for different reasons. They start with a confutation of natural law and finish with a legal foundation which differs from man's original nature.

The first consistent philosophical criticism of natural law which was no longer purely political as in the case of the members of the French Constituent Assembly, was utilitarian and can be found in Bentham's *Anarchical Fallacies*: a ferocious attack on the fanciful invention of rights which never existed, because for Bentham law is a product of the state's authority. 'Not truth but authority makes the law'. However, the authority which Bentham referred to was not an arbitrary power, because there existed an objective criterion which limited and therefore controlled authority, and that was the principle of utility, which Beccaria, who influenced Bentham, had already expressed in the formula 'the happiness of the greatest number'. Historicism was no less antagonistic to the concept of natural rights. For the more strictly legalistic version of the historicist school of jurisprudence, the law originated from the Spirit of the People, of all peoples, so each people had its own law, and the idea of a universal law was a contradiction in terms. For Hegel's philosophical version (although he opposed the historicist school as far as the need for a legal code in Germany was concerned), freedom and equality have little to do with nature and are in fact 'a product and a result of the historical mind', and for as long as they remain an abstraction they do not allow the concrete to emerge or they destroy it, the concrete being the organization of the state, a constitution and government in general'.

The rejection of natural law finally found its most radical expression in legal positivism, which was the prevailing doctrine among jurists from the first half of the last century to the end of the Second World War. Hans Kelsen and Carl Schmitt, the two most important German jurists of the first half of the century, adopted this position, even though they are usually considered representatives of two antithetical views of law and politics. For legal positivism, the natural rights being asserted are nothing more than subjective public rights, 'rights reflected' by the power of the state. They do not constitute a restriction on state power which preceded the birth of the state, but are in fact a consequence of the restrictions which the state imposes on itself, at least as far as Jellinek's famous doctrine is concerned.

There can be no doubt that the prolonged and repeated attacks on natural law through various arguments have left their mark. Today it would be difficult to advocate natural rights as in past centuries without theoretical revision or practical expedients. One can easily argue that there is no law except positive law without dismissing the needs which gave rise to the doctrines of natural law. These doctrines expressed in various ways the demands to correct, supplement and change positive law. The demands were given extra force by presenting them as 'rights', although they are not rights in the proper sense of the term: for jurists 'right' means a claim guaranteed by the existence of a superior power which is capable of compelling recalcitrants by force, a collective power which does not exist in the state of nature hypothesized by the exponents of natural law.

In spite of the criticisms against natural law, proclamations of human and citizens' rights have not only continued in the era of positivist jurisprudence, but have also continued to widen the scope of their demands to include the so-called social rights, and to break down abstract man into all his possible specifications, man and woman, child and old person, the healthy and the sick. The subsequent proliferation of charters of rights makes the four rights mentioned in the 1789 Declaration appear extremely narrow and wholly inadequate.

Finally the charters of rights have enlarged their area of validity from individual states to the international system. In the Preamble to the United Nations Statute promulgated after the tragedy of the Second World War, it was stated that human rights were from that time to be protected from outside and above the individual states, 'if it is to be avoided that man is compelled as a last resort to rebel against tyranny and oppression'. Three years later, the Universal Declaration of Human Rights was formally approved, and through it all people in the world ideally became subjects of international law and acquired a new citizenship, world citizenship, and therefore potentially have the right to demand enforcement of their rights against their own state. In that superb little book, *Perpetual Peace*, Kant outlines a system of law which goes beyond internal public law and external public law, and he calls it 'cosmopolitan right'. It is the law of the future which should no longer regulate the law between states and subjects or between individual states, but which should regulate the law between citizens of different states. It is a law which for Kant is not 'a fantastic expression of extravagant minds', but one of the necessary conditions for the pursuit of perpetual peace in a historical era in which 'a violation of rights in one part of the world is felt everywhere'.

The French Revolution has been exalted and execrated. It has been judged both a divine and a diabolic exploit. It has been considered either justified or unjustified for various reasons: justified, because it profoundly transformed European society, in spite of the violence that came with it; unjustified, because even a desirable end does not justify the means, and it is even worse when the end itself is not desirable or, although desirable, was never achieved. But however the events are judged, the Declaration still remains a milestone. Even Furet, whose interpretation and whose studies contributed to the idea that the Revolution has been over for some time, admits that 'the most spectacular demonstration of the restoration of the social contract was the Declaration of the Rights of Man', because it constituted 'the basis for a new way of living together'. The protagonists and contemporaries realized this themselves. On 8 August, Dupont de Nemours said: 'This is not a declaration of rights fated to last a few days. This is the law on which the laws of our nation and of other nations are founded, and it must last until the end of time.' At the end of 1789, Pietro Verri wrote in the *Gazzetta di Milano*: 'French ideas serve as a model to other men. While the rights of man were established in the mountains of the Alps, the marshes of the Low Countries and the island of Great Britain, these systems had little influence in the many other kingdoms. Enlightenment has now settled in the heart of Europe, and cannot help but influence other governments.'

I said at the beginning that the 1789 Declaration had been preceded by the American one. Very true, but it was the principles of 1789 which for over a century constituted an uninterrupted source of inspiration and ideals for people struggling for their freedom, and at the same time it was the principal object of derision and contempt for reactionaries of all confessions and factions who scorned that 'apotheosis of the high-flown bombast of the French Revolution: Justice, Fraternity, Equality and Liberty'. The historic significance of 1789 did not escape Tocqueville, although he was the first great historian to reject the way the Revolution saw itself: 'the period in which the declaration was drawn up was a time of youthful enthusiasm, boldness, generous and sincere passions, which in spite of all the errors, men would eternally recall, and which for some time yet would disturb the sleep of those who wish to enslave and corrupt other men'.

In one of the many counter-revolutionary documents by Pope Pius VI, who lived through the events, the right to freedom of thought and of the press was called a 'monstrous right . . . inferred from the equality and liberty of all men', and he commented that 'One cannot imagine anything more senseless than establishing such equality and liberty amongst us'. About two centuries later, Pope John Paul II sent a message to the Secretary of the United Nations for the thirtieth anniversary of the Universal Declaration, and he took the opportunity to demonstrate his constant interest and concern 'for fundamental human rights, whose expression we find clearly taught in the Gospel'. What better proof could there be of the victorious march of that text over its long history? If one leaves aside senseless and sterile factionalism, this victory seems to have led to the reconciliation of Christian thought with one of the highest expressions of secular and rationalist thought.

8 Kant and the French Revolution

In these times when the blind will to power that has dominated the history of the world has at its disposal extraordinary means by which to impose that will, it has never been more true that the scholar's task cannot be isolated from a renewed sense of responsibility in the twin meaning of the word. Being responsible means, on the one hand, realizing the consequences of your own actions, and on the other, answering for your own action before your fellow human beings. In other words, you should both avoid seeking refuge in the pure ethics of good intentions ('Do what you have to and let whatever is going to happen happen') and avoid shutting yourself up in splendid isolation ('I despise the sound of your harp which hinders me from listening to the voice of justice').

As our knowledge has increased and continues to increase at a bewildering speed, so our understanding of who we are and where we are going becomes ever more difficult. But at the same time, it is increasingly important, given the exceptional and incalculable dangers which threaten us. This contrast between the pressing need to grasp the confusion of problems in their totality – problems which have to be resolved to avoid unprecedented catastrophes – and the increasing difficulty in giving sensible answers to all the questions which would allow us to achieve that global vision which alone would ensure a peaceful and happy development of humanity is one of the paradoxes of our time. It is also one of the reasons for the difficulties which face the scholar who is eminently entrusted with the task of using his or her intelligence for clarification and leaving nothing undone in order to take on the challenge to reason which originates from uncontrolled passions and the mortal conflict of interests.

At the end of one of my recent speeches, I thought I could explain this 'uneasiness' of the man of reason (allow me not to use the word 'intellectual' which is now so worn out by over-use and sometimes incorrect use, and to which too often has been attributed the presumptuous and impossible task of finding Ariadne's thread in order to leave the labyrinth) by discussing the ambiguity of history.[1] History has always been ambiguous, in spite of appearances, because it has given different answers according to who was questioning it and in what circumstances. But today, following the extenuation of the idea of progress and the disappearance of a myth, it is more ambiguous than ever. The two interpretations that dominated the last century were Hegel's, which triumphed and which perceived history as the progressive realization of the idea of liberty (the Hegelian and clearly also the Marxian view of history as the transformation of the realm of need into the realm of liberty), and Nietzsche's catastrophic one according to which humanity is moving towards the age of nihilism. Today no one would want to hazard a guess or even bet on which of the two is destined to become true, nor would they see any point in it either. The human world is either going towards universal peace, as Kant predicted, or it is going towards a war of annihilation, and thus the word genocide has been coined in contrast to pacifism, one of the ideals of the century which believed in progress. The world is either moving towards the realm of liberty through the constant and widening scope of emancipation of individuals, classes and peoples, or it is moving towards the realm of Big Brother, as described by Orwell.

More generally, however, is there any point in asking oneself what history means? To ask oneself what history means is to believe that there is an intentionality in historical development, which has to be understood as a conscious direction towards an end. Any response to this question on the end of history has to involve the search for some pre-established plan attributable to Providence, Reason, Nature or the Universal Spirit. But no one can believe in a universal cause when modern thought is so fragmented, so diffident towards general ideas and, quite correctly in my opinion, so apprehensive about compromising itself with concepts that are too comprehensive. It can only be one of the many ways to anthropomorphize history, by attributing man's faculties and powers to an entity, in this case Humanity or Universal Reason, which differ from the individual man, through an analogical extrapolation which offers no guarantee of its veracity and only allows a purely conjectural reconstruction of history, to use a Kantian expression. But a completely conjectural history derived solely from indications but not substantiated facts would be, as Kant himself realized, like 'outlining the plot of a novel' or 'a simple distraction for the imagination'. This does not mean it is impossible to speculate on the course of history, as long as one is fully aware that although conjecture can fill gaps in our documentation between a distant cause and a recent effect, it would be completely illusory, and therefore vain, to reconstruct the entire history of humanity.[2]

For Kant prophetic history differed from conjectural history, and had a perhaps more ambitious aim, which was to discover a trend in the development of human history: whether it remains stationary, deteriorates or improves. (As is well known, the right answer for Kant was the last one). But prophetic history makes no claim to veracity as in the case of conjectural history. Unlike empirical history, which is the history of historians, prophetic history, which is the history of philosophers, does not proceed by causes, from one cause to its effect in an uninterrupted chain except to cover a few gaps by conjecture, but attempts to discover in an extraordinary event not so much the cause of a successive event as a clue, an indication, a sign (*signum rememorativum, demonstrativum, prognosticum*) of a tendency in humanity taken in its totality.[3] Only prophetic (or philosophical) history can challenge, if not exactly resolve, the ambiguity of historical development and give an answer to the question of whether humanity is in constant progress towards something better, while empirical history cannot, even if enriched by conjectural history.

Prophetic history can prognosticate, but it cannot predict. Prediction is the task of hypothetical history, whose propositions are formulated as 'if, thens', in a relationship between conditions and consequences, but it is not capable of establishing with any

certainty whether the conditions will occur which would necessarily lead to certain consequences. On the other hand, the extraordinary event which is the starting point for prophetic history, has
actually occurred. This kind of history can be made problematic
by the non-significance of the chosen extraordinary event, imping-
ing upon the credibility of the prophecy.

We can leave unanswered the question of whether Kant was
right in his choice of the event which showed humanity's trend
towards a better world. What matters to us today, in the bicen-
tenary year of the Revolution and all the commotion over 200-
year-old events which intensifies daily (and it has only just
started), is that the greatest philosopher living at the time chose the
French Revolution as the extraordinary event, the *signum prognosticum*, from which to draw his prophecy on the future of mankind.

Kant's famous writings on the French Revolution are to be
found in one of his last works, published in 1798, when the stormy
years which had shaken the world and lost the king his head were
already distant. The work, entitled 'A Renewed Attempt to
Answer the Question: "Is the Human Race Continually Improving", is the second part of *The Contest of Faculties*. It discusses the
conflict of the philosophical faculty, which Kant perceived as the
critical spirit, and yet he also perceived it as in the service of
reaction, and associated it with the smug enemies of the Revolution. As a leading authority has commented:

> Kant's faith in humanity's continual progress, in the profound
> rationality of history and in the final triumph of freedom and
> peace with justice, was never shaken, even after the disorders
> in France, the continuous wars of the period, and the wide-
> spread pessimism which was encouraged by jurists and states-
> men. It seemed to him that only the philosopher was able to
> understand the voice of history, measure the degree of human
> development, glimpse the future course of events, and show
> the way forward for civil and political reform.[4]

The essay was rejected as an apology for the Revolution, and was
only published after the death of Frederick William II in 1797,
when some of the restrictions on the freedom of the press were
lifted.

One paragraph is entitled 'An Occurence in our Own Times which Proves this Moral Tendency of the Human Race'. The event is 'the revolution . . . of a gifted people', and although it created such misery and cruelty as to discourage any right-minded person from attempting the experiment a second time, it affected the spirit of all the observers and they shared in its aspirations with a feeling akin to enthusiasm. This feeling was defined as 'the passion or enthusiasm with which men embrace the cause of goodness' and 'is always directed exclusively towards the ideal, particularly towards that which is purely moral'. It can have no other cause than 'a moral disposition within the human race'.[5]

The central point of Kant's thesis, and the one I wish to draw attention to, is that this moral disposition manifests itself in the affirmation of the natural right of a people not to be obstructed by other forces from establishing a civil constitution which it believes to be good. For Kant, this constitution could only be republican, the only one capable of avoiding the principle of war. He believed that the Revolution's strength and morality consisted in this right of a people to establish freely their own constitution in harmony with the natural rights of single individuals, so that those who obey the laws must also be convened to enact the laws. The very concept of honour, which belonged to the ancient nobility and warrior class, perishes before those who come armed with the vision of their people's rights.

Some of these ideas had already been expressed more fully in two previous works: *Idea for a Universal History with a Cosmopolitan Intent and Perpetual Peace*. The former, which was written in 1784, and therefore a few years before the Revolution, went unnoticed at the time, even by those, like Hegel and Fichte, who knew and commented on the latter work. Like all Kant's other works on the philosophy of history, it was opposed by historicists, from Dilthey to Meinecke, who considered history as a pattern or the teleological concept of history to be a left-over from the anti-historical philosophy of the Enlightenment. It was not until the beginning of this century that some socialist philosophers influenced by Kant got round to reassessing these works.[6] Criticisms revolved around the question of whether or not the philosophy of history was a legitimate discipline, the aporetic nature of Kant's philosophy of history, and the extent of its consistency with Kant's other

works. However, less importance was given to the work's central
theme which was the trend in human history towards a world-
wide legal order, a theme which Hegel may have derided, but
which has never been so relevant as it is today. This theme of a
universal civil society, which is so well expressed by the key term
Weltbürgertum, originated with the stoics, but was transformed by
Kant from a naturalistic concept into a teleological concept of
history.

Kant was well aware of the fact that it is conflict, not peace,
which spurs on progress. However, he also realized that there is a
point where antagonism becomes excessively destructive and
some form of self-regulation is required for conflict, even in the
form of a universal civil code. In a period of continuous warfare
between sovereign states, he lucidly observed that 'the savage
liberty' of existing states:

> through wars, through excessive and never remitting prepara-
> tion for war, through the resultant distress that every nation
> must, even during times of peace, feel within itself, they are
> driven to make some initial, imperfect attempts; finally, after
> much devastation, upheaval, and even complete exhaustion of
> their inner powers, they are driven to take the step that reason
> could have suggested, even without so much sad experience,
> namely, to leave the lawless state of savagery and enter into a
> federation of peoples.[7]

The critics of Kant's philosophy of history also failed to notice that
this concept of the *universal civil society*, by which every person is
potentially a citizen not of a single state but of the world, was
further developed in *Perpetual Peace* (1795). One of the aspects of
this work which has been least studied is Kant's introduction of a
third category of law which he called *jus cosmopoliticum* (cosmopolitan right), alongside the more traditional categories of internal and external public law. As is well known, the imaginary
treaty of perpetual peace was made up of three definitive articles:
the first, which stated that the constitution of every state had to be
republican, belonged to internal public law; and the second,
which stated that international law must be founded on a federa-
tion of free states, belonged to external public law. However,

Kant's third definitive article read: 'Cosmopolitical right shall be limited to conditions of universal hospitality'.[8]

Why did Kant feel the need to add a third form of public law to the two traditional internal and external forms? The reason was that he not only felt that one should take into consideration relations between a state and its citizens and between a state and other states, but also relations between every individual state and citizens of other states, and inversely between a citizen and a state other than his own. As far as the first relationship is concerned, this means the duty of hospitality or right (for Kant emphasized that this was a right and not merely a philanthropic duty) of a foreigner to arrive in a country and not be treated in a hostile manner. As far as the second relationship is concerned, this means 'the right of resort, for all men are entitled to present themselves in the society of others by virtue of their right to communal possession of the earth's surface. Since the earth is a globe, they cannot disperse over an infinite area, but must necessarily tolerate one another's company'.[9] Two state duties derive from these two rights of the citizen of the world: firstly, the duty to permit a foreign citizen to enter one's own territory, thus censuring the inhabitants of the Barbary Coast who captured ships which landed there and enslaved their crews and passengers; and secondly, the duty of a guest not to take advantage of the hospitality in order to transform the visit in conquest, thus censuring the European mercantile states which sent in troops to oppress the indigenous population on the pretext of establishing trading posts. (It is perhaps worth remembering that Hegel who ridiculed Kant's fantasies of perpetual peace, justified colonial expansion.)

Kant's reciprocal relationship between the foreign citizen's right to visit and the visited states' hospitable duty pointed the way to the right of every man to be a citizen not only of his own state but the entire world, and he represented the whole earth as a potential city of the world, that is a universal civil society.[10] Kant put the finishing touches to his general system of law and completed his description of the history of law, once he had established this last type of relationship between states and individuals from other states, and not just between individuals, between a state and the individuals within it, or between one state and another. This fourth and last stage concerned a universal legal system based on a law

122 Kant and the French Revolution

between individuals, as in the state of nature when there was no law but private law, with the civil state governed by internal public law and international order governed by external public law. Kant did not perceive cosmopolitan right, which was to be the last stage in the process, as the product of extravagant minds, because 'the peoples of the earth have . . . entered . . . into a universal community, and it has developed to the point where a violation of rights in one part of the world is felt everywhere', and thus cosmopolitan right was 'a necessary complement to the unwritten code of political and international right, transforming it into a universal right of humanity. Only under this condition can we flatter ourselves that we are continually advancing towards a perpetual peace.'[11]

It is no longer controversial that the Universal Declaration of Human Rights of 10 December 1948 laid the foundations for giving individuals and not just states legal recognition under international law, and therefore started the transition to a new stage of international law, from the rights of all peoples to the rights of all individuals. Perhaps this new stage of international law should be called cosmopolitan right, in recognition of Kant's contribution.

Kant made no reference to the French Revolution in his work on perpetual peace. Only in his last work, which I referred to at the beginning, in which he took up again the question of a civil constitution founded on the right of a people to make its own laws the sole basis for a system which could eliminate war for ever, did he acknowledge the great event in France as history's prophetic vision, a premonition of a new world order.

The interpretation given by the greatest philosopher of the time is worthy of a place among the many ways of celebrating this event, especially as his interpretation is the only one that conserves its perennial value and rises above historical polemic which often cannot see the wood for trees.

When faced with the ambiguity of history, I too believe that one of the few, perhaps the only sign of a credible movement towards a better world is the increasing interest among educated people in human rights and the international appeals for their wider recognition and more effective guarantees.

A premonitory sign does not constitute proof. It is simply a reason for not remaining passive spectators, and not encouraging through our passivity those who say 'the world will always continue as it has in the past'. This attitude, as Kant said, 'contributes to the fulfilment of their own prediction' that the world does in fact go on as it has in the past.[12] The price of indolence is high!

Notes

1 'La pace ha un futuro?', a lecture given at the International Symposium of the City of Lugano on 'The Future of Peace and Violence of the Future' (18–20 November 1987), and published in *Il terzo assente* (Turin: Edizioni Sonda, 1989), pp. 188–94.
2 I. Kant, *Mutmasslicher Anfang der Menschengeschichte*, 1789; *Conjectures on the Beginning of Human History*, in *Political Writings* (Cambridge: Cambridge University Press, 1991), p. 221.
3 Kant, 'Ob das meschliche Geschlecht in beständigen Fortschreiten zum Besseren sei' (1797), 'A Renewed Attempt to Answer the Question: "Is the Human Race Continually Improving?" ', in *Political Writings*, p. 181.
4 V. Mathieu, 'Nota storica', introducing I. Kant, *Scritti politici e di filosofia della storia e del diritto* (Turin: UTET, 1965), p. 87.
5 Kant, 'A Renewed Attempt to Answer . . .', *Political Writings*, pp. 182–3.
6 I took this information on the changing fortunes of Kant's writings on the philosophy of history from M. Mori, 'Studi sulla filosofia kantiana della storia', *Rivista di filosofia*, vol. LXX (1979), pp. 115–46.
7 Kant, *Idea for a Universal History with a Cosmopolitan Intent*, in *Perpetual Peace and Other Essays*, trans. T. Humphrey (Indianapolis/Cambridge: Hackett, 1983), p. 34.
8 Kant, *Perpetual Peace* in *Political Writings*, ed. Hans Reiss, trans. N.S. Nisbet (Cambridge: Cambridge University Press, 1991), p. 105.
9 Kant, *Perpetual Peace*, in *Political Writings*, p. 106.
10 My attention was drawn to the theme of cosmopolitan right in Kant, as the introduction to a new phase in the development of human law by D. Archibugi, 'La democrazia nei progetti di pace perpetua', *Teoria politica*, vol. VI, no. I (1990), pp. 122 ff; and 'Le utopie della pace perpetua', *Lettera internazionale*, vol. V, no. 22 (autumn 1989), pp. 58–9.
11 Kant, *Perpetual Peace*, in *Political Writings*, pp. 107–8.
12 Kant, 'A Renewed Attempt to Answer . . .', in *Political Writings*, p. 178. Finally, for the relationship between Kant and the French Revolution, see C. Rosso, 'Kant e la rivoluzione francese. Molte rivoluzioni in una', *Alma Mater Studiorum* (Bologna University), vol. II, no. 2 (1989), pp. 65–76, and particularly interesting is the book by D. Losurdo, *Autocensura e compromesso nel pensiero politico di Kant* (Naples: Bibliopolis, 1983).

Part III

9 Against the Death Penalty

1. Whether we like it or not, we have to accept that, in relation to the millennia of human history, the debate over the abolition of the death penalty has barely begun. For centuries, the question of whether it was lawful (or just) to condemn the guilty to death was not even posed. It was never doubted that the death penalty should be one of the punishments inflicted on those who transgressed the laws of tribe, city, people or state, and indeed the death penalty was the prince of punishments which most fully satisfied the community's need for retribution, justice and security from its contaminated members. We can start with Plato's *Laws* or *Nómoi*, the first great book on laws and justice in our Western civilization. Plato dedicates a few pages in Book IX to the question of penal laws. He recognizes that 'no penalty imposed by the law has an evil purpose . . . it makes the person who pays the penalty either more virtuous or less wicked', but adds that in the case of the death penalty, if 'the judge should consider him as already beyond cure . . . the very tiniest of evils will be what the offender suffers'.[1] I am not going to list every crime for which this book recommends the death penalty, but it is for a very wide range – from crimes against deities and religion to crimes against parents or voluntary homicide. Of the premeditated murderer, Plato states that he will be 'ineluctably obliged to pay the penalty prescribed by the law of nature – to suffer the same treatment as

he himself meted out to his victim'.[2] I draw the reader's attention to the adjective 'natural', and the principle of 'suffering' that which has occurred. This principle of talion or 'an eye for an eye' was more ancient than Plato and the Pythagoreans, and was to be taken up by medieval jurists and repeated for centuries according to the famous expression by which *malum passionis* must correspond to *malum actionis*. It runs through the entire history of criminal law, and is still very much with us. As we shall shortly see, it is one of the most common justifications for the death penalty.

I have quoted this famous ancient text simply to provide the most authoritative demonstration of how the death penalty has been considered not only perfectly legitimate, but 'natural' since the very beginning of our civilization, and it has never been a problem to accept it as a punishment. I could have quoted many other texts to show this. Indeed, the death penalty has constituted so little a problem, that the practice of capital punishment was never seriously challenged even by a religion of non-violence and *noli resistere malo*, which raised the question of conscientious objection and the obligation to carry arms, especially in the early centuries, and whose divine inspiration came from a man condemned to death.

2. It was not until the Enlightenment at the heart of the eighteenth century that the legitimacy and appropriateness of capital punishment was discussed in any depth *for the first time*, which is not to say that the question had never been raised before. The historic importance of Beccaria's book (1764), which cannot be emphasized too much, was precisely this: it was the first work to deal with the problem seriously and provide rational arguments for a position which contrasted with the centuries-old tradition.

It has to be said straight away that the starting point for Beccaria is exclusively the question of the punishment's deterrent effect. 'The purpose [of the punishment] is solely to prevent the guilty party from inflicting further injury to citizens and deterring others from doing similar deeds'.[3] We shall see later that this starting point was extremely important in the development of the theme. If this is the basis for the punishment, it is a matter of knowing the relative deterrent effect of the death penalty. This method of argument is still used today, and has been used by

Amnesty International on several occasions. Beccaria's response can be found in the principle he introduces in the paragraph entitled the 'Mildness of Punishments'. This principle is the following: 'One of the greatest obstacles to crime is not the cruelty of punishments, but the likelihood of their being inflicted, and consequently the vigilance of magistrates and the thoroughness of an inexorable judge which in order to be effective should be accompanied by mild legislation'.[4] Thus moderation in punishment. Punishments do not have to be cruel in order to deter. It is sufficient for them to be assured. It is not so much the severity of the punishment as the certainty of being punished at all which constitutes a reason, indeed the principle reason, for not committing a crime. Beccaria then introduces a second principle: the deterrent arises not from the intensity of the punishment, but its duration, as in the case of life imprisonment. The death penalty is very intense, while life imprisonment is long-lasting. Thus the perpetual loss of one's own liberty has greater deterrent effect than the death penalty.

Both Beccaria's arguments are utilitarian, in the sense that they challenge the usefulness of the death penalty (he commences his argument with the expression 'neither useful nor necessary').[5] Beccaria added another argument which has caused some puzzlement (and has in fact been largely abandoned). The so-called contractualist argument is based on the theory of social contract and an original agreement of civil society. This argument can be summarized as follows: if civil society is based on an agreement between individuals who renounce living in the state of nature and create laws for their mutual protection, it is inconceivable that these individuals would have also given their peers control over their own life.

The incredible success of Beccaria's book is well known, and that fame was largely due to Voltaire's extremely favourable reception of it. Beccaria was a nobody, while in France, the land of enlightenment, Voltaire was Voltaire. It is equally renowned that the debate that opened up around the death penalty during that period led to the proclamation of the first criminal law abolishing the death penalty: the Tuscan law of 1786 which, following a series of considerations once again on the deterrent effect but not neglecting the corrective role of punishment ('the correction of the criminal who is also a child of society and the state'), declared in Clause 51 'the abolition for ever of the death penalty for any criminal, whether condemned in his presence or absence, and whether having confessed and having been convicted of any crime punishable by death in previously promulgated laws, which in this matter we hereby declare abolished'.[6]

The book's influence in Catherine II's Russia was perhaps even more extraordinary, and her famous *Instruction* which was issued as early as 1765 and therefore only a year after the publication of Beccaria's book, states: 'The experience of all centuries proves that the death penalty has never improved any nation'. This is followed by a sentence which appears to have been taken word for word from Beccaria's book: 'If then I can show that in ordinary civil society, the death of a citizen is neither useful nor necessary, I will have furthered the cause of humanity'.[7]

3. One should add, however, that, in spite of the literary success of the book among the educated public, not only was the death penalty not abolished in the countries which considered themselves civilized in relation to other historical periods and countries that were considered barbarian or even savage, but the cause of abolition was not even to prevail in contemporary penal philosophy. I could give many quotations, but will confine myself to three from the most important thinkers of the time: Rousseau in *The Social Contract* (published in 1762, two years before Beccaria's book), the great Kant and the even greater Hegel. In the chapter of *The Social Contract*, entitled 'The Right of Life and Death', Rousseau rejected the contractualist argument. He argued that it was not true that the individual reserved the right to his own life in all cases when he agreed with others to establish the state: 'it is in order that we may not fall victim to an assassin that we consent to die if we ourselves turn assassins'.[8] Thus assigning the right to one's life to the state serves not to destroy it but to protect it from others.

A few years after the publication of Beccaria's *On Crimes and Punishments*, another important political thinker, Filangieri wrote the *Science of Legislation* (1783), the greatest Italian work on political philosophy in the second half of the eighteenth century, and in it he accused Beccaria's contractualist argument of 'sophistry'. He argued that yes, man does have a right to life in the state of nature, and it is also true that he cannot renounce that right, but he can lose it through his crimes. If he can lose it in the state of nature, one cannot see why he should not lose it in civil society, which was constituted not to create a new law, but precisely in order to ensure the exercise of the ancient right of the offended party to react and meet force with force, to repulse an attack on one's own life with an attack on another's life.

Kant and Hegel, the two greatest philosophers of the time, one before and one after the French Revolution, both upheld a rigorously retaliatory theory of punishment and came to the conclusion that capital punishment was even an obligation. Kant, starting with the concept of punishment as retribution, perceived the function of punishment purely as legal redress and not the prevention of crime. In other words, the punishment had to correspond precisely to the crime (this is justice as a kind of equality, which the ancients called 'corrective equality'). He argued that the state had a duty to apply the death penalty, and this was a categorical imperative, not a hypothetical imperative based on a relationship between means and end. I quote directly from the text, choosing the most significant sentence:

> If he has killed, he *must* die. There could be no substitute or commutation of sentence which would satisfy justice. No *comparison* can be made between a life, however troubled, and death; and consequently no other redress between the crime and the punishment other than death lawfully inflicted on the criminal, but without any cruelty to the patient which might disgust humanity.[9]

Hegel goes even further. After having rejected Beccaria's contractualist argument on the basis that a state cannot be created by a contract, he argues that the criminal not only must be punished in a manner which corresponds to his crime, but has the right to be punished with death, because only punishment can redeem him and only punishing him can one recognize him as a rational being (in fact Hegel says it 'honours' him). He does add however that Beccaria's work did at least have the effect of reducing the number of capital punishments.[10]

4. It was unfortunate that while the greatest philosophers of the time continued to support the legitimacy of capital punishment,

one of the major supporters of its abolition was none other than Robespierre in a famous speech to the Constituent Assembly in May of 1791, precisely the man who went down in history during the period of restoration (the period in which Hegel wrote his work) as the person most responsible for the reign of terror and indiscriminate executions (of which he too fell victim, as though to prove the inexorable law that revolutions devour their own children, violence generates violence, etc.). Robespierre's speech should be remembered, because it contains one of the most persuasive arguments condemning the death penalty. He started by rejecting the death penalty's deterrent effect, claiming that it was no more of a deterrent than other punishments, and cited the almost ritual example of Japan, as Montesquieu had done earlier: at that time it was believed that Japanese punishments were extremely brutal and yet Japan was full of criminals. He also rejected the argument based on the people's consent and of course the one based on redress. Finally he introduced the argument, which Beccaria overlooked, that judicial errors are irreversible. The whole speech is inspired by the principle that mild punishments are a proof of civilization (and here the influence of Beccaria is evident), while cruel punishments are a sign of barbarity (Japan again). It would hardly be an exaggeration to say that the most famous and intelligent proponent (almost imitator) of Beccaria was Robespierre, and more's the pity.[11]

5. In spite of the persistence and prevalence of the anti-abolitionist theories, it cannot be said that the debate over the death penalty which Beccaria commenced, has been without effect. The opposition between abolitionists and anti-abolitionists is too simplistic and does not exactly reflect reality. The debate over the death penalty did not aim solely at its abolition, but primarily at its limitation to a few serious and clearly defined crimes, the elimination of the sufferings (or pointless cruelties) which so often accompanied it, and an ending to ostentatiously public events. When we deplore the continued existence of the death penalty in the majority of states, we tend to forget the enormous step forward which has taken place in the legislation of almost all countries over the last two centuries, which has decreased the number of offences punishable by death. In England at the beginning of the nineteenth century, there were more than 200 crimes punish-

able by death, which included crimes which are now punished by a few years of prison. Even in those legal systems where capital punishment survives, it is inflicted almost exclusively for premeditated murder. Apart from the reduction in capital offences, there has also been a relaxation in the obligation to inflict it in cases where it applies, and judges and juries have been given greater discretionary powers. As far as the cruelty of execution is concerned, one only has to read Foucault's fascinating book *Discipline and Punish* which, in the chapter entitled 'The Spectacle of the Scaffold', describes some horrifying episodes of executions preceded by drawn-out and vicious tortures. An English author, writing in the eighteenth century and quoted by Foucault, speaks of the tormented death sentence as the art of keeping the victim alive in suffering, dividing death into a thousand deaths, and inducing the most sophisticated agonies before life ceases. The torment is thus the death sentence many times over: as though capital punishment was not enough, sophisticated forms of execution kill the victim again and again. Torment responds to two requirements: it must dishonour the victim (through the scars it leaves on his on her body and the screams that accompany it), and it must be a spectacle, one which is viewed by everybody.

This question takes us back to public spectacle and the need to make the executions public (public spectacles did not disappear once public executions were eliminated, because there were also parades of chained convicts in public before they were sent to forced labour). Today the majority of states which have retained the death penalty, carry it out with the discretion and reserve of a painful duty. Many non-abolitionist states have attempted not only to eliminate the torments, but also to make the death penalty painless as far as is possible (or at least less cruel). Naturally this does not mean they have succeeded: one only has to read accounts of the most common forms of execution, the French guillotine, the English gallows and the American electric chair, in order to understand that it is not entirely true that suffering has been eliminated, because death is not always so instantaneous as we are led to believe or as those who support the death penalty would like us to believe. In any case, it has been removed from the public gaze, although the echo of an execution in the press replaces the public presence in the square before the scaffold, and we should not

134 Against the Death Penalty

forget that where the freedom of the press exists there is wide circulation of scandal sheets. On the shamefulness of public executions, I will just recall the invectives of Victor Hugo who fought strenuously against the death penalty all his life, with all the power of his eloquent style (although today it might appear grandiloquent). A collection of Victor Hugo's writings on the death penalty has recently been published in France: a veritable mine of quotations. The book shows how he fought against this punishment from his youth to his old age, as a politician and then through his writings, poems and novels. His invectives always start with the description of an execution. He wrote in *Les Miserables*: 'The scaffold, when it is there, rising up before you, is something awe-inspiring. Until you have actually seen a guillotine, you can be indifferent to the death penalty and not form an opinion either way. But when you see one, it makes a violent impression and you have to decide whether you are for or against'. He remembered that at the age of sixteen, he saw a woman convicted as a thief whom the executioner branded with red-hot metal: 'I still have the woman's terrified scream in my ears after more than forty years. She was a thief, but for me she became a martyr from that moment on'.[12]

I wished to call the reader's attention to how the death penalty has evolved in order to demonstrate that the Enlightenment debate has not been without effect, even though the death penalty has not been abolished. I should also like to add that very often when a court does pronounce the death sentence, it is not actually carried out. In the United States, the case of Gary Gilmore who was executed in January of 1977 in the state of Utah, caused an outcry because no one had been executed since 1967. In 1972, a famous ruling by the Supreme Court established that many of the circumstances in which the death penalty was applied were unconstitutional, on the basis of the Eighth Amendment which prohibits the infliction of cruel and unusual punishments. However, in 1976 another decision changed this interpretation and claimed that the death penalty does not always violate the constitution, thus opening the way for another execution, which was to be Gilmore's. The fact that the death sentence provoked so much discussion and revived the abolitionist associations shows that even in those countries where capital punishment still exists, there is a watchful and sensitive section of public opinion which hinders its application.

6. It is fairly clear from what I have said so far that the arguments for and against the death penalty depend almost always on the role attributed to punishment. There are two principal concepts: the concept of retribution based on the rule of justice as equality (as we have seen in Kant and Hegel or correspondence between equals, according to the maxim that it is just that whoever carries out an evil action is treated in the same way as he treated others (the law of talion, like for like or Dante's famous *contrappasso*) and by which it is just (or justice requires) that he who kills is himself killed (he who does not respect life has no right to it, he who has taken the life of another loses the right to his own, etc.); and the concept of prevention, according to which the purpose of punishment is to discourage with the threat of something unpleasant any action which a given legal code considers harmful. On the basis of this concept, it is self-evident that the death penalty is only justified if it can be proved that its deterrent effect is greater than any other punishment (including life imprisonment). These two contrasting concepts of punishment can also be termed *ethical* and *utilitarian*, and they are based on two different ethical theories, the first on the ethics of principles or justice, and the second on the utilitarian ethic which has prevailed in recent centuries and still prevails in Anglo-Saxon countries. You could say in general that anti-abolitionists appeal to the former (e.g. Kant and Hegel) and the abolitionists to the latter (e.g. Beccaria).

Allow me to narrate a historical episode, which often comes up in a debate like this. It is taken from Thucydides' *Histories*, and goes right back to 428 BC.[13] The Athenians had to decide the fate of the inhabitants of Mytilene who had rebelled, and two orators spoke. Cleo argued that the rebels should all be sentenced to death, as they had to be paid back in kind and punished as they deserved. He also added that other allies would know that rebels would be punished with death. Diodotus, on the other hand, argued that the death penalty served no purpose, because 'it is impossible – and whoever thinks otherwise is very naive – for human nature, when it has embarked enthusiastically on some project, to be checked by the force of the laws or some other threat, and thus one should avoid putting too much faith in the death penalty as a sure guarantee in preventing evil'.[14] He went on to suggest that they should adhere to the principle of utility and, rather than kill the people of Mytilene, they should make them their allies.

7. In reality the debate is a little more complicated, because there are more than these two concepts of punishment (although these two are by far the most prevalent). I shall refer to just three more: punishment as atonement, as reparation and as defence of society. The first of these is more favourable to abolition of the death penalty than its conservation: in order to atone for one's crime, one has to live. But one could also argue that the true atonement is death, perceiving death as the purification of guilt and the elimination of the stain: blood is washed away with blood. Strictly speaking, this concept of punishment is compatible with both the maintenance and the abolition of the death penalty.

The second concept of reparation is the only one which totally rules out the death penalty. Even the most perverse criminal can redeem himself: if you kill him, you remove all possibility of moral improvement, which should not be refused to anyone. When Enlightenment figures argued for the replacement of the death penalty by forced labour, they justified their argument by stating that work redeems. In his comment on Beccaria's treatise, Voltaire referred to Catherine II's penal policies which were favourable to abolition: 'Crimes have not multiplied because of this humanity, and it almost always occurs that when the guilty are exiled to Siberia, they then become good people'. And a little later he adds: 'Force men to work, and you will make them honest persons.'[15] (One could argue at length over this ideology of work, whose most extreme, abominable, macabre and evil consequence appeared in the writing over the entrances to the Nazi concentration camps: *Arbeit macht frei*, 'Work makes you free'.)

The third concept of defence of society is also ambiguous. Generally those who have argued that the purpose of punishment is to defend society have been abolitionists, but they have supported this argument for humanitarian reasons (partly because they reject the concept of guilt which is the basis for the concept of retribution, which can only be justified in terms of free will). However, the defence of society does not preclude the death penalty: one could argue that the best way to defend society from its most dangerous criminals is to eliminate them.

8. Although there might be several theories of punishment, the two principle ones are what I have termed the ethical and utilitarian theories. It is, moreover, a distinction which goes beyond two different perceptions of punishment because it refers to a deeper ethical (or moral) distinction between two different methods for judging good and evil: one based on good principles whose validity is absolute, and the other on good results, meaning results which bring the greatest good to the greatest number, as utilitarians like Beccaria and Bentham argued. It is one thing to say that you must not do evil because there is a rule which prohibits it (for example the Ten Commandments), and quite another to say one must not do evil because of the harmful effects on human society. These are two distinct criteria which do not coincide, because it is quite possible for an action which is judged bad in terms of principles to have good consequences from a utilitarian point of view, and vice versa.

As we have seen in this dispute for and against the death penalty, those in favour follow an ethical concept of justice and the abolitionists follow a utilitarian theory. Reduced to their bare essentials, the two arguments could be summarized by the statements: 'the death penalty is just' and 'the death penalty is not useful'. For the former argument it is just, regardless of its utility. Kant's reasoning from this point of view is faultless: to consider the person condemned to death to be a deterrent is to turn a person into a means or, today we would say, to exploit him. For the latter argument, it is not useful, regardless of its justness. In other words, for the former, the death penalty might not be useful, but it is just, and for the latter, it might be just, but it is not useful. Therefore, for those who hold to the theory of retribution, the death penalty is a necessary evil (and perhaps even a good thing as we have seen with Hegel, because it restores the order which has been violated). For those who hold to the theory of deterrence, the death penalty is an unnecessary evil, and so can never be considered a good thing.

9. There can be no doubt that since Beccaria, the principle argument of abolitionists has been the deterrent effect. Yet the statement that the death penalty has less deterrence than forced labour

is a matter of personal opinion, itself based on a psychological assessment of a criminal's state of mind which is not supported by factual proof. Ever since there has been a positivist approach to criminology, there has been empirical research into the comparative deterrence of punishment, and crime rates have been compared for different places and times, with and without the death penalty. These studies have, of course, been assisted in the United States where in some states the death penalty is in force and in others it has been abolished. In Canada, the Moratorium Act of 1967, which suspended the death penalty for five years, has made it possible to study crime levels comparing the present with the past. A very careful examination of these studies shows that in reality none has produced results which are totally convincing.[16] There are, in fact, so many related variables which have to be taken into account, apart from the simple relationship between a decrease in punishments and an increase or decrease in crime. There is, for example, the likelihood of the punishment, the problem posed by Beccaria: which is the greater deterrent, the gravity of the punishemnt or the likelihood of its infliction? Only if the likelihood remains stable in both periods, can a comparison be made. This was the case with Italian terrorism: which contributed more to the defeat of terrorism, the more severe penalties or the improvement in the means for discovering terrorism?

Given the indecisive results of these studies, we often take refuge in opinion polls (the opinions of judges, criminals under death sentence or the public at large). But just to start with, majority opinion is not valid in matters of good and evil, as Beccaria himself knew:

> To those who argue that nearly all centuries and nearly all nations have inflicted the death penalty for some crimes, I would reply that this argument falls apart in the face of the truth, against which it has no appeal. Human history gives us the impression of a great sea of errors, above which a few confused truths float divided by great distances.[17]

In the second place, opinion polls prove very little, because they are subject to the mood of the people and the emotive effect of events. It is well known that public attitudes to the death penalty shift according to the level of social tension. If it were not for terrorism and the increase in crime in recent years, the question of the death penalty would probably not even be posed. Italy was one of the first states to abolish the death penalty (Zanardelli Penal Code, 1889), and when Croce wrote his *History of Italy* in 1928, he asserted that the abolition of the death penalty had become a way of life and the very idea of its restoration was irreconcilable with national sensitivities. Yet a few years later, fascism reintroduced the death penalty without greatly upsetting public opinion, leaving aside the futile protests of a few anti-fascists. Of these, I wish to recall *La pena di morte e la sua critica*, written by Paolo Rossi in 1932, who later became a minister in the Republic and President of the Constitutional Court. The author forcefully condemned the death penalty, principally using the reparation argument.

The weakness of the argument for the abolition of the death penalty based on its lesser deterrence is that if it could be proven incontrovertibly that death, at least in certain circumstances, does have greater powers of dissuasion than other punishments, then it would have to be maintained or restored. One cannot escape the seriousness of this objection. I therefore believe that the exclusive use of the utilitarian argument in favour of abolition, while not totally mistaken, does have grave limitations.

It is true that there are secondary arguments, but they are not in my opinion decisive. There is the argument of the irreversibility of the death penalty, and therefore the impossibility of rectifying judicial errors. But anti-abolitionists can always reply that it is precisely because capital punishment is so severe and final that it should only be inflicted where there is absolute certainty of guilt. In this case, it would be a matter of introducing a further restriction on its application. If, however, the death penalty is just and is a deterrent, it does not matter if it is applied only in a few cases; the important thing is that it exists. There is also a counter-argument concerning those who revert to crime. Marcel Normand has recently written a work (1980) on the death penalty in the popular series *Que sais-je?*, the last I have had a chance to read. The author fiercely defends the death penalty, and uses the argument about the repetition of crimes. He refers to some cases, which I must admit are impressive, of murderers condemned to death and then pardoned, who in spite of many years of prison, commit other

murders on release. Thus the disturbing question: if the death
sentence had been carried out, would it have saved one or more
human lives? The conclusion is that society sacrifices innocent
lives in order to save the life of a criminal. The author's leitmotif
is the following: abolitionists take the side of the criminal, and
anti-abolitionists the side of the victim. Who is right?

10. However the question I previously put in relation to the
utilitarian theory is even more embarrassing: the theory's weakness is that it is based purely and simply on the presumption that
the death penalty does not assist in reducing violent crime. And
what if it were possible to prove it could prevent crimes? Here
then the abolitionist must appeal to another argument of a moral
nature, to a principle which is absolutely indisputable (a truly
ethical postulate). This argument can only come from the moral
imperative: 'Thou shalt not kill', perceived as an absolute principle. But it could be argued that if the individual has the right to
kill in self-defence, then so must the community. The reply is that
the community does not have this right, because legitimate
defence can only be justified as an immediate response where it is
impossible to do otherwise. The community's response has to go
through a sometimes lengthy procedure, in which the arguments
for and against are debated. In other words the death sentence
following a legal procedure is no longer killing in self-defence, but
a legalized, cold-blooded and premeditated murder. The killing
requires an executioner, i.e. a person authorized to kill. It is not
unsurprising that the executioner, although authorized to murder, was considered a monstrous person. Charles Duff's *Handbook
on Hanging* depicts the executioner grotesquely as a dog, society's
faithful friend. It also refers to the case of an executioner who
became a murderer and had to be executed, thus rebutting the
deterrent effect of the death penalty.[18]

The state cannot act in the same way as the individual. The
individual acts out of anger, passion, self-interest or self-defence.
The state responds meditatively and rationally. It too has a duty
to defend itself, but it is so much stronger than the individual that
it has no need to snuff out a single life in order to defend itself. The
state has the privilege and benefits of a monopoly of force. It must
recognize the responsibilities of this privilege and these benefits.
I know very well that this is a difficult and abstract argument

which could be accused of naive moralism and useless preaching. Let us try to give a reason for our repugnance for the death penalty. There is just one reason: the commandment not to kill.

I can see no other reason. Apart from this last reason, all the other reasons are worth little or nothing, and can be rebutted with other arguments which have more or less the same persuasive force. Dostoyevsky put it magnificently through the words of Prince Myshkin: 'It is said: "Thou shalt not kill". So why then if someone kills, does he too have to be killed? To kill someone who has killed is a punishment which far surpasses the crime itself. Legal murder is incomparably more horrible than murder by villains.'

Moreover, because this last reason for condemning the death penalty is high-principled and difficult, the great majority of states will continue to apply the death penalty, in spite of the international declarations, the appeals, the abolitionist societies and the laudable activities of Amnesty International. Nevertheless, we firmly believe that the total disappearance of the death penalty from the world theatre is destined to be an incontrovertible sign of human progress. John Stuart Mill (an author whom I love) expressed this very well: 'The entire history of social improvement has been a series of transitions, by which one custom or institution after another, from being a supposed primary necessity of social existence, has passed into the rank of a universally stigmatised injustice and tyranny.'[19]

I am convinced that this will also be the destiny of the death penalty. If you ask me when we will achieve this destiny, I have to reply that I do not know. I only know that the achievement of this destiny will be an incontrovertible sign of moral progress.

Notes

1 Plato, *The Laws*, trans. by T. J. Saunders (London: Penguin, 1970), pp. 357–8 (854 e).
2 Ibid., p. 386 (870 e).
3 C. Beccaria, *Dei delitti e delle pene*, ed. F. Venturi (Turin: Einaudi, 1965), p. 31. This edition also documents the incredible success of the book in eighteenth-century Italy and Europe.

4 Ibid., p. 59.

5 Ibid., p. 62.

6 The quote from the *Riforma della legislazione criminale toscana del 30 novembre 1786* is translated from the text which appears in Beccaria, *Dei delitti*, ed. Venturi, p. 274.

7 From the sixth question in the *Instruction*, which appears on p. 646 of *Riforma della legislazione criminale*. In the Preface to his book, Venturi speaks of Catherine II as a faithful plagiarist of Beccaria (p. xxxv).

8 J.-J. Rousseau, *The Social Contract*, trans. G. D. H. Cole (London: Dent, 1973), II, V, p. 190.

9 I. Kant, *The Metaphysic of Morals*, in *Political Writings*, p. 156.

10 The reference to Beccaria can be found in § 100 of *Philosophy of Right*. An appendix to § 100 states that: 'Beccaria's efforts to abolish the death penalty did produce some advantageous effects; even if neither Joseph II nor the French ever managed its total abolition, there has been more awareness of which crimes are punishable and which are not'.

11 Robespierre concluded his speech by stating: 'Il faut croire che le peuple doux, sensible, généreux qui habite la France, et dont toutes les vertus vont être développées par le régime de la liberté, traitera avec humanité les coupables, et convenir que l'expérience, la sagesse vous permettent de consacrer les principles sur lesquels s'appuie la motion que je fais que la peine de mort soit abolie'. The quotation is taken from M.A. Cattaneo, *Libertà e virtù nel pensiero politico di Robespierre* (Milan: Istituto Editoriale Cisalpino, 1968).

12 *Écrits de Victor Hugo sur la peine du mort*, ed. Raymond Jean (Paris: Éditions Actes/Sud, 1979).

13 This episode appears in bk III which deals with rebellion and punishment in Mytilene in 428–427 BC.

14 This passage comes from §§ 45 and 46 of bk III.

15 From Voltaire, *Commentaire sur le Traité des délits et des peines* 1766), and also appears in Venturi, p. 374.

16 C.H.S. Jayewardene, *The Penalty of Death* (Toronto: Lexington Books, 1977).

17 Beccaria, *Dei delitti . . .*, p. 68.

18 Charles Duff, *Handbook on Hanging* (London: Cayme Press, 1928), revised edition (London: Putman, 1961).

19 J.S. Mill, *Utilitarianism*, in *Utilitarianism, Liberty, Representative Government*, ed. H.B. Acton (London: Dent, 1972), ch. V, p. 59.

10 The Current Debate on the Death Penalty

1. In a world like ours which is ravaged by increasingly cruel and destructive civil and international wars, by the spread of increasingly savage, devious and merciless terrorist acts, and is resigned to living under the threat of nuclear extermination, the debate over the death penalty whose effects are not even remotely comparable to the massacres which occur every day, might appear little more than an idle pastime for the same old pundits who fail to understand how the world works.[1]

I refer of course to the death penalty following due legal procedure, which is the particular subject of this essay. There is nothing to be said about the extra-judicial death penalty in all its forms, whether inflicted by death squads, secret services, the police under the shield of self-defence, persons unknown (who must remain unknown) in prison where a prisoner is serving a sentence other than the death penalty, or indirectly in a concentration or labour camp (there is no moral distinction between killing and intentionally leaving to die). It can only be condemned as an atrocity, and all its aspects should perhaps be studied in order to understand its reasons, discover the circumstances which favour it, and explain its growth. There can be no greater condemnation of the extra-judicial death penalty than the pages of the book still very much remembered by members of my generation: *Letters by Those Awaiting Execution during the European Resistance.*[2]

The long-running debate over the death penalty revolves around the question of whether it is morally and/or juridically permissible for the state to kill in order to punish, even with all the procedural guarantees of a constitutional state. In other words, it is a question of whether the state's right to punish, which is not generally challenged, extends to the right to inflict the death sentence, even as part of a legal process. The problems raised by extra-judicial killings are completely different. No one is expecting a new Beccaria to appear, denounce their inhumanity, and propose their abolition with humanitarian ('the mildness of punishment') and judicial (the limitations on the social contract) arguments. These are problems which belong to a different chapter of moral and juridical philosophy, the chapter relating to the justification of war or the exercise of violence by individuals or groups in conflicts where there is no guiding principle other than self-protection. It is clear that once it is admitted that war is legitimate in certain circumstances, and therefore that a conflict can be resolved through the use of weapons, then a licence to kill is admissible within certain limits (constituted by *jus belli*). As far as extra-judicial killings are concerned, the ethical and/or juridicial problem is not whether it is legitimate to inflict the death sentence, but whether it is legitimate to resort to any kind of extra-judicial punishments within a properly constituted state, and if so, with what restrictions and in what circumstances.

2. The debate over the death penalty is recent compared with the many centuries that have passed since the birth of Western philosophy. In 1764, Beccaria wrote the work which sparked the great controversy among the learned over the arguments for and against capital punishment. The first state to abolish it was the Grand Duchy of Tuscany in 1786. Along the whole course of philosophical history, the general opinion among philosophers was favourable to the death penalty, starting with Plato and going far beyond Beccaria: one only has to think of Kant, Hegel and Schopenhauer. If we were to base our argument on the great authorities, the abolitionists would be defeated.

I shall ignore here the ambivalent influence of Christianity on the question (it is ambivalent in that according to the times and the circumstances, different arguments for and against have been drawn from the same religious vision of the world). As far as the great philosophical concepts of society and the state are concerned, the organic concept of the state which dominated the ancient and medieval worlds, and the related Aristotelian principle that 'the whole precedes the parts', offered one of the most common arguments for justifying the death penalty. If man as a political animal cannot live outside the society of which he is logically a member, then the life or rather the survival of that society in its totality is a more important asset than the life and survival of its parts, particularly an individual's life which must be sacrificed for the life of the whole, when it is diseased because it risks infecting and endangering the life of the whole. For centuries the source text was the following passage by St Thomas Aquinas:

> Now every part is directed to the whole, as imperfect to perfect
> . . . For this reason we observe that if the health of the whole
> body demands the excision of a member, through its being
> decayed to the other members, it will be both praiseworthy
> and advantageous to have it cut away. Now every individual
> person is compared to the whole community, as part to whole.
> Therefore if a man be dangerous and infectious to the community, on account of some sin, it is praiseworthy and advantageous that he be killed in order to safeguard the common
> good.[3]

In order to demonstrate how persistent this argument has been in the defence of the death sentence, let me just refer to the reasoning used by Naphta in Thomas Mann's *The Magic Mountain*. This 'revolutionary conservative' argues against Settembrini who has just concluded his impassioned discourse against the death penalty, with these words: 'As soon as something above the person and the individual is in the balance, then not only is the individual life sacrificed without ceremony for higher thoughts, but even the individual spontaneously offers up his life, and this is the only state worthy of man.'

It is no coincidence that the first abolitionist theories, starting with Beccaria, developed in the context of an individualistic concept of the society and the state, which completely inverted the relationship between the whole and the parts, and made possible, from Hobbes onwards, the concept of a state founded on a social contract. Beccaria was not only a contractualist but, as is well known, used the precisely the contractual origins of the state as one of his arguments. The denial of a state's right to punish the guilty by death certainly cannot be claimed as the logical conclusion to and therefore necessary part of any theory that traces the origins of the state to a social contract. The best proof is the existence of thinkers who were both contractualist and non-abolitionists (the most famous example being Rousseau, and we could add our own Filangieri). But unlike the organic concept which thinkers have generally used to justify the death penalty, the contractualist concept made its rejection possible, if not obligatory. In § 100 of *Philosophy of Right* in which he defends the death penalty, Hegel uses his criticism of Beccaria as the pretext for one more argument against social contract theories which he profoundly disliked.

3. Although relatively recent, abolitionist theories have had considerable success, if not in terms of total abolition, given that there are far more states which maintain it than have abolished it, at least in terms of partial abolition. I do not think it superfluous to underscore yet again that what we are now debating is the *final* abolition of the death penalty, which these days is restricted in the states which maintain it to an increasingly small number of particularly serious crimes. There is no longer any disagreement over the need to limit its legislative application: the death penalty has long ago ceased to be the principal punishment, as it was for centuries, given that it was considered easy to carry out as well as being the greatest deterrent (indeed the only really effective deterrent). One might say that the majority of legislators before the great Englightenment debate agreed with Draco who, when asked about the reasons for his severity, replied that the death sentence was just for petty thieves, and that unfortunately he had not discovered heavier punishments for more serious crimes. After Beccaria, it was not only questioned whether the death penalty was legitimate ethically, but also whether it really was the greatest punishment.

To give some idea of the gradual delegitimization of the death penalty, three factors should be taken into consideration:

1 The number of crimes for which the death sentence is mandatory is decreasing, while the number of crimes for which the death sentence is left to the discretion of the judge and jury is increasing.
2 The death sentence is not carried out in all the countries in which capital punishment remains on the statute books. Thus all the reports on the situation concerning the death penalty list those countries where it has been abolished *de facto* as well as those where it has been abolished *de jure*.
3 Even where the death penalty remains on the statutes and the death sentence has been passed, there has been a tendency towards suspension *sine die* and pardons.

While there has been a clear reduction in the death penalty in the long period since the Enlightenment, both in the number of states that inflict it and in the types of crime, two other factors must be specified in order to give the full picture. Firstly, the gradual conquests of the abolitionists have been halted before the last fortress, which is putting up implacable resistance against total abolition. Consequently the debate for and against the death penalty cannot be considered over, and the abolitionist cause is far from won. Secondly, this tendency towards abolition, when considered over short periods rather than long, proves to be anything but clear-cut, and sometimes seems to proceed in fits and starts.

As far as the status of the debate is concerned, it is worth remembering that it is considerably more heated in countries where total abolition has not yet occurred and the problem is *de iure condendo*, or where the reform has only recently been introduced. In a country like Italy where following the fall of fascism, the abolition of the death penalty was restored and in fact constitutionalized, for the moment at least there is much less evidence of a return to traditional anti-abolitionist doctrines, particularly in relation to the United States and France. When I speak of 'doctrines', I refer to the debate among philosophers, sociologists, psychologists, jurists, etc. The argument shifts for what is called 'popular sentiment' or the 'common sense' of Anglo-Saxon authors. It is, in fact, often noted by those who discuss this subject that there is a considerable difference between popular and expert opinion over the question of the death penalty. Abolitionism is

now prevalent among those associated professionally with the
problem, in the human rights organizations and even in the established churches (contrary to a tradition which appeared to be
solid), while if we are to believe the opinion polls, although there
are serious doubts over their reliability, popular sentiment continues to be hostile to abolition or even demands restoration in
countries where it has been abolished for some time. As I have
spoken of Italy, I could hardly fail to mention that while the
educated have not yet shown any sign of raising the problem of
the increase in criminal and political violence and its increasingly
vicious nature, public opinion has proved to be sensitive to these
matters, as can be inferred from letters to newspapers, everyday
conversations, and the response to extreme right-wing movements and parties. The fact that this difference between expert
opinion and popular opinion exists is proven by one of the weaker
arguments which anti-abolitionists resort to in order to sustain
and substantiate their arguments in those countries where the
debate is most intense. This is the so-called 'common-sense' argument. The minister Rocco used it to justify the restoration of the
death penalty in Italy under fascism. However the argument is
weak for several reasons: (a) the popular invocation of the death
penalty ('shoot the lot of them') is indiscriminate, making no
distinction between the more and less serious crimes; (b) popular
sentiment is fickle, being easily influenced by circumstances; and
(c) questions of principle do not lend themselves to solutions
based on majority rule.

In relation to the second observation concerning the irregular
development of abolitionism, the main observation which has to
be made is that legislation governing the death penalty reflects the
greater or lesser tension within a given society and the (often
subsequent) greater or lesser degree of authoritarianism in the
regime. Thus while the overall tendency in the long term is towards limitation of capital punishment both *ratione loci* and *ratione
materiae*, there are cases in which the death penalty is restored for
a brief period where it had been abolished for years: the case of
Italy under fascism is typical. The dependence of the death penalty debate on the state of public order is confirmed by the fact
that in Italy during the period in which the Zanardelli Code
abolishing the death penalty (1889) was on the statute book, the

question of its restoration was never seriously raised under conditions of gradual containment and regulation of social conflict, but when it was restored by an authoritarian regime like fascism, partly because of the worsening social conflict immediately following the First World War, it occurred with the public's consent or at least its indifference. If there was any resistance, it took a purely doctrinal form, given the widespread conformism (Paolo Rossi's book, which appeared in 1932, should be remembered in this context).

4. The particular intensity of the current debate over the death penalty arises not only from the continued interest in a legislative solution to the question, but also because it has become part of one of the debates which has most taxed contemporary moral philosophers (especially in Anglo-Saxon countries): the debate on the right to life. To get an approximate idea of the breadth and importance of this debate, one should consider that, apart from right to life in the limited sense, i.e. the right not to be killed, it includes the right to be born or to be left to come to life, the right not to be left to die, and the right to be kept alive or the right to survival. Given that there is no right for one individual without a corresponding duty for another, and given that every duty requires an imperative regulation, the debate over the four forms which make up the right to life leads into a debate over the validity of and possible limitations on the duty not to kill, not to abort (or procure an abortion), to assist anyone whose life is in danger, and to offer the minimum requirements for survival to anyone who lacks them. Translated into legislation, these four duties presuppose four imperatives, of which the first two are negative (or commands not to act in a certain manner) and the other two positive (or commands to act in a certain manner).

As far as the right to life is concerned, the question of the death penalty comes under the general debate on the right to life in the strict sense, and subsequently on the validity of and possible limitations on the rule 'do not kill'. For those who believe that 'do not kill' has an absolute validity, and is therefore in the Kantian sense a categorical imperative which does not allow for exceptions, the problem of the death penalty has already been resolved: it is not legitimate to inflict the death penalty. But are there any categorical imperatives? Kant himself was a supporter of the death penalty. So 'do not kill' is not a categorical imperative? Fortunately we do not have to reply to this question, as in reality the debate over the legitimacy of the death penalty is showing no signs of abating and continues to feed increasingly subtle controversies between moral philosophers. This means that none of the contendents starts from the premise of the absolute validity of the precept 'do not kill', or consequently from the perception of the right to life as an absolute right which must be applied in all cases, without exception. The so-called fundamental rights, which certainly include the right to life, are characterized by their universality; that is to say, they are valid for every person, irrespective of race, nationality, etc., but not necessarily to be applied without exceptions.[4] I do not want to suggest that there are no absolute rights (examples in the modern consciousness are, I believe, the right not to be tortured and the right not to be held as a slave), but am simply stating that the absoluteness of the right to life is not usually used in favour of the abolition of the death penalty (and besides it would be difficult to do so). Having admitted then that the commandment 'thou shalt not kill' does allow for exceptions, the controversial point is whether the death penalty can be considered an exception. As it is a general rule in all controversies that those who defend an exception to a general principle, have to justify it, it is for the supporters of the death penalty to produce the arguments that would make it admissible, and for those who reject the death penalty to refute them. Procedurally the debate over the death penalty has involved, since its inception until the present day, the prior presentation of arguments to justify this exception to the prohibition on killing, and the successive defence of the precept, at least in specific cases.

5. The two most common (and easy) arguments for justifying the death penalty are *necessity* and *self-defence*, just as in the centuries-old debate on the justification for the use of force, which becomes a search for the *justa causa* for behaviour which would normally be considered unjust. The most historically interesting example of this, which can still teach us a great deal, is the question of a just war. As everyone knows, *necessity* and *self-defence* justify a crime (with a subsequent immunity from accusation or punishment), and are admitted under the criminal law of all countries. It is therefore argued that surely what is valid for the indi-

vidual should also be valid for the state. Indeed it is more justifiable for the state, because of the supremacy of the state over the individual which gave rise to the doctrine of the *reason of state* which prospered for so many centuries. This principle admits the suspension of general norms in the conduct of the state which could not be allowed in individual behaviour. Naturally these two reasons for justifying an extremely serious act by the state such as murder, can also be considered from the individual's point of view, as he or she holds the universal right to life, which derives from the equally universal obligation not to kill. If we start with the premise that the right to life is not an absolute right (just as the precept not to kill is not absolute), it follows that it can be lost. (Another problem is whether one can renounce the right to life, and whether the right to life is accompanied by the duty to live.) There are two circumstances in which it can be lost: when it conflicts with a fundamental right which is considered superior, and when the holder of the right does not acknowledge and violates the equal right of others, or in other words when it clashes with *another* right or the right of *another*. All things considered, necessity and self-defence could be used to justify the death penalty on the grounds of the individual's right (but not absolute right) to life: according to the justification based on necessity, the individual's right to life conflicts with the security of the state; according to the justification based on self-defence, the individual loses the right to life for having endangered the lives of others, for whom the public authorities act as avenger.

However, they are both weak arguments: I have referred to them because in spite of their tenuousness they are frequently used, although now more as *common sense* than as philosophical doctrine. Their weakness derives from the fact that we are not faced with the dilemma of either inflicting the death penalty or letting a criminal act go unpunished. The death penalty or legalized killing is only one of the possible punishments available to the state. One cannot discuss the legitimacy or appropriateness of the death penalty without taking into account that it is not the only remedy for crime and there are alternative punishments. Both necessity and self-defence are justifications based on the premise that the individual has no alternative in certain circumstances in which he or she could not avoid breaking the law (necessity transcends the law) or his or her life is seriously threatened. The state, which has a monopoly over the use of force, does not usually find itself in these situations (while an individual policeman could, but he, like any other citizen, can benefit from the extenuating circumstances of self-defence): the state is endowed with alternative punishments and is not therefore obliged to inflict this punishment.

When these alternative sanctions, which include severe punishments like life imprisonment, are unavoidably taken into account, then the whole debate about the death sentence shifts to a comparison between it and its alternatives. It is no longer a disputation on the justifications for breaching the precept 'do not kill', taken in isolation and therefore as an *absolute,* but rather a debate in the presence of specific practical alternatives to the death penalty, and therefore *in relation* to them. In other words, it is no longer simply a question of the legitimacy and appropriateness of the death penalty as murder with a just cause, but the legitimacy and appropriateness of legal murder in competition and therefore in relation to other sanctions. Advocates of the death penalty cannot confine themselves to arguments in favour of the suspension of the precept not to kill (such as necessity and self-defence), which would be valid for individual action and in the case of war, where the state does not have access to alternative effective sanctions, such as detention, against other states but must present arguments to justify legal murder *in spite of* the fact that the state has other available means for punishing the guilty (and therefore for preventing crime). When Beccaria made the first spectacular pronouncement condemning the death penalty, one of the arguments used which was to prove most effective was that life imprisonment has a greater deterrent effect than death, and therefore in relation to life imprisonment, the death penalty was 'neither useful nor necessary'.

6. Once the death penalty has been removed from the debate over possible suspensions of the precept 'do not kill' and transferred to the strictly penal dispute over the nature and function of different punishments which the state can use to carry out its punitive and preventive responsibilities – thus perceiving the death penalty as a sanction and as one of the available sanctions, and as such a means for punishing the guilty (*quia peccatur*) and

for hindering similar crimes in the future (*ne peccatur*) – there are two principle theories which still have to be challenged with 'good reasons': the theory of retribution according to which the essential purpose of punishment is to repay a *malum actionis* with a *malum passionis*, and the preventive theory, according to which the essential purpose of punishment is to discourage actions which the statutes consider harmful, and which must therefore constitute a deterrent.

There is a clear distinction between the two theories, although in practice some people may draw on arguments from both in order to support their position. Generally, however, the majority of those who support the theory of punishment as retribution advocate the death penalty, while the advocates of abolition are mainly to found among those who support the theory of punishment as prevention. The distinction is clear-cut because the two theories are based on a different general approach to the problem. Two different questions can be posed in relation to the death penalty, as with any other action which the state might take in absolving its duties: (a) whether it is ethically legitimate; and (b) whether it is politically opportune. The two questions must be kept distinct, because they can lead to different responses: a course of action which is ethically just could be politically inopportune, and vice versa. The age-long conflict between ethics and politics originates from this distinction. As has been observed many times, the conflict between ethics and politics is in reality a conflict between two kinds of ethic (which Max Weber called the ethic of intention and the ethic of responsibility), or if you like two different criteria for judging the goodness and evil of human actions: either in accordance with the universal principles whereby it is assumed that good acts must be prescribed and bad acts forbidden, or in accordance with the result obtained which is usually judged on the utilitarian principle of the greatest happiness of the greatest number of people (thus the conflict between the two ethics is portrayed as a conflict between deontological morality and utilitarian morality). Well, the question posed by the advocates of retribution is whether the death penalty is morally legitimate, and thus they put themselves in the ethical position of judging actions on the basis of pre-established principles; on the other hand, the question posed by the advocates of prevention is whether the death penalty is politically opportune, and thus they put themselves in the ethical position of judging actions on the basis of results.

I wanted to draw attention to this distinction in the general approach to the problem because it helps to explain why the debate between proponents of retribution and prevention so often seems like a dialogue of the deaf. Asking oneself whether a guilty person should be condemned to death because it is just is a problem concerning the ethics of principles or moral legitimacy; while asking oneself whether the death penalty should be inflicted because it is a greater deterrent than any other punishment is a problem concerning the ethics of results or political opportunity.

This divergence in premises is the best proof of one of fundamental arguments used by both sides not to support their own theories but to refute their opponents'. Kant, who advocated the death penalty on the basis of retribution, rejected the deterrent argument as immoral, because it violated the precept that people should not be used as a means. The utilitarian, being convinced that the penalty is useless because it is less of a deterrent than other punishments, rejects the retribution argument as the result of obtuse and inhuman moral rigour.

In summary then, those who perceive the death penalty as a question of justice, have to demonstrate that the death penalty is just on the basis of the principles of justice through retribution (which is a sub-species of justice in general, on a par with commutative and arithmetic justice), independent of any reference to social utility (*fiat iustitia, pereat mundus*). Those who have a purely utilitarian perception of the death penalty, reject it because it does not serve the ends which the state must set itself, as it is not an ethical body, and those ends are the discouragement of crime, irrespective of any argument based on abstract justice. For the former, the death penalty might even be useful, but what matters is that it is just. For the latter, it might well be just, but what matters is that it is useful. As they do not think it is useful, it has to be rejected as an unnecessary evil, while for the others, it satisfies a need for justice and therefore has to be approved of, because it is morally good, irrespective of whether or not it is useful.

7. The divergence in philosophical premises is certainly one of the reasons why the debate is never entirely exhausted, but always alive, intense and persistent, with the opposing sides never admitting defeat. But it is not the only reason. It should be remembered that a debate on moral philosophy does not belong to the field of demonstrative logic, but to that of argumentative logic and rhetoric (to use Perelman's expression), and therefore the arguments for and against do not invalidate each other and are not definitive. There is no argument brought by one side which is not rebutted by the other. There is not a 'good' reason presented in defence of one theory which is not counterbalanced by a 'good' reason in defence of the opposite theory.

Consider the following: the theory of retribution whose strength lies in its appeal to the principle of just retribution or commutative justice, according to which one of the rules on which any society is founded is the correspondence between giving (or doing) and receiving (an application of the general principle of reciprocity), has its weakness in the assertion that the only possible correspondence to inflicting death is receiving death. Kant argues that whoever kills must die (and it is a categorical duty, not a hypothetical one) and 'no possible substitute can satisfy justice. For there is no parallel between death and even the most miserable life, so that there can be no equality of crime and retribution unless the perpetrator is judicially put to death.'[5] In using this argument, he is taking for granted that death is the worst of all evils. But what if this were not the case? Certainly when Kant says that there is no comparison between a life however troubled and death, he means to refute Beccaria's theory and anybody who followed him. But his is an unqualified statement without any proof.

At this stage, the theory of retribution is obliged to abandon its heavenly principles and come down to earth. It has to deal with empirical data, and go down the rather dangerous and uncertain path of the so-called 'preference' argument (as used by Feuerbach and many others since): if given the choice of death or life imprisonment, which would a condemned man choose? There can be no doubt that the advocate of retribution is obliged to follow this line of argument because his theory stands or falls on whether he can prove which punishments are just for which crimes (and for murder which is the most serious crime, the just punishment must be the most severe punishment). But it is equally certain that the preternece argument has, in my opinion, been disproved on several occasions, both because an argument like this has to be supported by an enormous sample of different people, a difficult task which has never been seriously undertaken, and because the choice between immediate death and death deferred until the end of what will probably be a long period of detention is not between alternatives which are emotionally comparable, the first being certain and precluding all hope and the second leaving room for hope or the illusion that the situation might improve in the long term. The fact that a condemned man declares a preference for a long period of detention is not so much proof of the greater fearfulness of the death penalty, as the expression of a person's mood, from which no conclusion can be drawn.[6]

The weakness in the prevention theory, which now prevails among abolitionists (given that traditionally the legitimacy of the death penalty has been argued by advocates of the retribution theory), is that it puts all or almost all its money on the one horse: deterrence. Its principal argument is that the death penalty does not have the deterrent effect that has (arbitrarily) been attributed to it, and therefore lacks its only *raison d'être* from a utilitarian point of view. The weakness of this argument is that up till now there has been no definite proof on the deterrent effect of different punishments, particularly the death penalty in relation to long periods of detention, in spite of the opinion polls and empirical research in those countries where the death penalty has either been abolished or restored, between 'before' and 'after'. In this field too, the social sciences have been stuck in the universe of approximation. Of course it is not the fault of social scientists, but the almost infinite variety of those entities (human beings) which constitute the object of their observations, and the changing conditions in which individuals operate, so that it is difficult to make the same observation with all other things being equal. There are many variables which have to be taken into account, the most important of which being the extraordinary variety of crimes and motives, and the likelihood of being discovered and punished. This was the problem posed by Beccaria: which has greater deterrence the severity of the punishment or its likelihood of being inflicted? Comparison is possible only if the likelihood remains stable in both moments 'before' and 'after'. The question has been asked repeatedly in the debate over terrorism and in relation to kidnapping in Italy: which would contribute more to the defeat of terrorism and a reduction in kidnappings – the introduction of more severe sentences or increased efficiency in the fight against crime? Powerful criminal organizations like the Mafia obtain extraordinary obedience to their laws through the threat of the death penalty (the only penalty they know), because the probability of avoiding the penalty is minimal for anyone who disobeys them.

Such is the doubt surrounding the deterrent effect of the death penalty in relation to long periods of detention, that some abolitionists have been obliged to fall back on a wager (like Pascal's with the equal chance of winning and losing): both maintenance and abolition are based on a wager, in the sense that the proponents are betting on its effectiveness, and the adversaries on its ineffectiveness. But there is a difference in the wagers: to bet on effectiveness leads to a result which cannot be reversed if the doubt is resolved in favour of the opposing argument, but to bet on ineffectiveness by saving a life allows a reversal should it be discovered that one's position is erroneous. The wager argument remains provisional for as long as there is any uncertainty over the question: is the death penalty or life imprisonment more of a deterrent? While the plausibility of Pascal's wager derives from the fact that the doubt over the existence of heaven and hell is a radical doubt which is humanly insoluble, the abolitionists' wager is based on a doubt which could be resolved, though if resolved against them, one which would signify their definitive defeat. This leads to the conclusion that if one wants to plant the abolitionist theory on solid ground, one cannot restrict oneself to the deterrent argument, because one would have to admit defeat, if it were proven irrefutably that the death penalty has a greater deterrent effect than other punishments, which is by no means impossible, at least in certain situations and for certain crimes.[7]

8. The truth is that a theory, especially a theory in the moral and political field, should not be defended by a single argument. Consider what happens in a court room: apart from what lawyers call a principal argument, there is a subordinate argument followed by an incidental argument. The literary genre which

writings on moral philosophy come closest to (and increasingly so) is that of the lawyer summing up his or her case: you expound the adversary's arguments and for each one, you present an objection and anticipate any counter-arguments for which you present further objections, and so on.

The controversy over the death penalty is no exception. A report based on two questionnaires sent by the United Nations to governments, non-governmental bodies and representative persons in the 1960s listed fifteen reasons given by abolitionist states of which the first was precisely the argument that 'the value of the death penalty as a "deterrent" was not proven or was arguable', supported by the belief that imprisonment was sufficient and 'reinforced' by the observation that in some cases the death penalty was itself the cause of crime.[8] There is no need to repeat them all, especially as some only concerned the country the replies came from. There is not a single one to which the anti-abolitionists have not countered or could easily counter with an opposing argument. I shall examine only two of these counter-arguments as they seem the most important historically (and are still so today). One is philosophical and the other more strictly juridical.

The two general concepts of punishment which I have dealt with are concepts based on retribution and the utilitarian concept. Both perceive punishment in terms of the tasks and interests of the state. But the problem of punishment can also be considered from the point of view of the individual who must be subjected to them. From this point of view, the most common concepts are atonement and reparation. In the first case, the purpose of punishment concerns not the punisher but the punished, who has to contribute to the redemption of the evil act through his or her suffering, and in the second case, it is to assist the condemned person to correct the wrong, and through correction, to rehabilitate him- or herself. Now, of these two concepts, the first is entirely compatible with the death penalty, because one could argue that it is not possible to atone for the most serious of all crimes, the murder of a fellow being, other than by death perceived as the purification of guilt and the cancellation of the stain (blood is washed away with blood). The second concept, on the other hand, is absolutely incompatible with the death penalty for the obvious reason that the necessary condition for correction is survival. There is a clear correspondence between these two concepts of punishment from the culprit's point of view and the two concepts from the public authority's point of view. The argument based on atonement can be used to reinforce the case for the death penalty, and the argument based on reparation to reinforce the case for abolition. However, both are irrefutable in their own terms, because they are based on axiological premises which, if not based purely on emotions, are rooted in complex belief systems that are difficult to compare.

The abolitionists' strongest legal argument is that the execution of the death penalty makes any judicial error irreparable. No treatise on the death penalty fails to refer to cases in which proof of an alleged criminal's innocence was discovered after his on her death on the scaffold. It has never seemed acceptable that the social cost of the death of an innocent is outweighed by the benefit to society from the physical elimination of so many vicious criminals: indeed it is an argument from which human conscience generally recoils in horror. Even leaving aside the easy response of anti-abolitionists that the death penalty should be applied with the utmost caution and only when there is absolute certainty of the crime on the basis of the wise maxim 'it is better that a criminal is saved than an innocent dies' (given that if the death penalty is just and efficient, it does not matter if it is seldom applied, what does matter is that it exists), there is an argument against abolition which is at least as strong as the one of judicial error. Anti-abolitionists can point to numerous cases of recidivous murderers, that is to say dangerous criminals who have committed other crimes after being released at the end of their term of imprisonment or following an escape.[9] There can be no doubt that cases of criminals reverting to crime do raise this disturbing question: 'If they had been condemned to death, wouldn't innocent lives have been saved?' If we accept the maxim 'it is better that a criminal is saved than an innocent dies', what do we say about: 'it doesn't matter if an innocent dies, as long as a criminal is saved'? The question is embarrassing even when the victim of the recidivist is not an innocent in legal terms, as in the cases of revenge for an actual injury, and is therefore legally indictable. One cannot avoid this question, given the startling frequency with which murders continue to be perpetrated by common criminals and terrorists who would probably have been executed in countries where the death penalty is still in force.

Finally, the death penalty debate involves not only these arguments bouncing back and forth, but also reversible or double-edged arguments, which can be used by either side. A rather curious example of this concerns the 'harshness' of the death penalty, which for its opponents constitutes a humanitarian reason for its abolition. On the other hand, a philosopher who certainly could not be accused of being a conservative, John Stuart Mill, gave a speech in the English Parliament in favour of the maintenance of the death penalty for the most serious crimes, because abolition would have produced 'an enervation, an effeminacy in the general mind of the country', discouraging contempt for death which society relies on as a necessary social virtue.[10] But the most interesting example of inversion concerns the different use of the precept 'do not kill'. The advocates of the death penalty often resort to the argument that capital punishment for murder is the solemn consummation (the most solemn that there is) of the commandment not to kill, in the sense that the life of a fellow human being must be respected if one's own life is to be respected. For the abolitionist on the other hand, capital punishment is an unacceptable violation of the obligation not to kill. This concept cannot be expressed better than in the words Dostoyevsky puts in the mouth of Prince Myshkin at the beginning of the novel, almost as an introduction to his hero: 'To kill someone who has killed is a punishment which far surpasses the crime itself. Legal murder is incomparably more horrible than murder by villains.' On the one hand, the commandment not to kill is used to justify the death penalty and on the other to refute it.

9.   The debate over the death penalty, which I have attempted to summarize briefly, will continue. Let no one think that the definitive victory (I mean 'definitive') of its opponents is close. One of the few assured and unchanging lessons of history is that violence engenders violence, not only in practice, but what is even more serious, with all the ethical, juridical and sociological justifications which precede and follow it. There is no violence, even the most ruthless, which has not been justified as the response, the only possible response, to the violence of others: the violence of rebels as the response to the violence of the state and the violence of the

state as a response to that of the rebels, and so on in an endless chain, just as family and private vendettas can form endless chains.

During this essay I have been mainly referring to the violence of the common criminal. One should not forget that political violence occupies a much larger position in the wider historical theatre, and this political violence includes collective violence and war, compared with which talk of 'abolitionism' as in the case of the death penalty, might appear unforgivable naivety. One cannot ignore political violence, because it gives rise to conti- nuing demands for the death penalty and the use of killing even by the state, although generally in all those extra-judicial forms I referred to at the beginning. It was only during the growth of the liberal and constitutional state during the last century that there arose a tendency to consider the political moti- vation of violent acts against the institutions of a state (especially a despotic state which is therefore neither liberal nor constitu- tional) with a certain indulgence, while for centuries a political crime, a crime of lese-majesty, was treated with the utmost severity. Now we are faced with an explosion of political terror- ism, the trend has been reversed even in liberal and constitutional states, and the clearest evidence of this is the passing of special legislation.

We must not create false hopes. On the other hand we must not forget how much has already been achieved: enormous strides have been made, of which we are not always fully aware. From the origins of human society until so recently that it is practically yesterday, the mark of state power has been power over life and death. Elias Canetti commented in his incisive reflections on sur- vival as a manifestation of power (my survival depends on your death, *mors tua vita mea*):

No-one may come near [the autocrat]; a messenger or anyone who has to approach him, is searched for weapons. Death is systematically kept away from him, but he himself may and must decree it. He may decree it as and when he wills and his sentence will always be executed; it is the seal of his power, and his power is absolute so long as his right to decree death remains uncontested.[11]

And on the last page: 'The threat of death is the coin of power.'[12] He gives a profusion of terrifying examples of the extensiveness and the frequency of this power in all eras and in a great variety of places. Of an African kings, he wrote: 'All his commands had to be obeyed absolutely, to disregard any of them meant death. Here the command manifests itself in its oldest and purest form, as the death sentence with which the lion threatens weaker animals.'[13]

I draw my strongest argument against the death penalty from the fact that violence engenders violence in an endless chain reaction, perhaps the only argument for which it is worth fighting. The salvation of humanity, now more than ever, depends on the interruption of this chain. If it is not broken, the day might not be far off when an unprecedented catastrophe occurs (some people not without reason have spoken of a final catastrophe). So we must start. The abolition of the death penalty is only a small beginning. But it will be a great and radical transformation in the practice and perception of state power, traditionally portrayed as irresistible power.

Notes

1 The literature on the death penalty is immense, but also repetitive. I will limit myself here to citing two volumes (which together come to some thousand pages) because I rarely see them referred to: *Pena de morte*, the proceedings of the conference *Coloquio internacional do centenario da abolicão da pena de morte en Portugal*, (Coimbra: Faculty of Law of the University of Coimbra, n.d. but the conference took place in 1967). These two volumes not only contain a review of the situation in relation to the death penalty in different countries, but also an analysis of the arguments for and against by some of the greatest contemporary jurists and philosophers of law. Naturally the Amnesty International report, *The Death Penalty* (London: Amnesty International Publications, 1980) is fundamental.
2 *Lettere dei condannati a morte della Resistenza*: one of the fuller versions was edited by P. Malvezzi and G. Pirelli and published by Einaudi in 1954, with a preface by Thomas Mann.
3 Thomas Aquinas, *Summa Theologica*, II, II, qu. 64, art. 2. See also Taparelli, *Saggio teoretico di diritto naturale* (1848), § 840.

4 On this point, I should like to draw attention to a book by J.S. Fishkin, *Tyranny and Legitimacy. A Critique of Political Theory* (Baltimore and London: Johns Hopkins Press, 1979), in which it is argued that a principle of government which is applied without exceptions ends up legitimizing what the author defines as 'tyranny'.

5 I. Kant, *The Metaphysic of Morals*, in *Political Writings* (Cambridge: Cambridge University Press, 1991), p. 156. For Kant and criminal law, see an important recent monograph by M.A. Cattaneo, *Dignità e pena nella filosofia di Kant* (Milan: Giuffrè, 1981).

6 This is without mentioning cases in which the condemned man has preferred the death sentence to be executed. There has been the recent case, which caused a bit of a stir, concerning Frank J. Coppola, an ex-policeman condemned to death for killing a woman during a robbery, who in spite of his protestations of innocence up to the last minute, rejected all attempts to postpone his execution, asserting his firm decision to die 'in order to safeguard his own dignity and save his family from further anguish and pain'.

7 The 'preference' and 'wager' arguments were suggested to me by an article by D.A. Conway, 'Capital Punishment. Some Considerations in Dialogue Form', *Philosophy and Public Affairs*, vol. 3, no. 4 (1974) pp. 431–43.

8 *Capital Punishment* (New York: UN Dept. of Economic and Social Affairs, 1962), pp. 30–1.

9 There was the particularly sensational case of Louis Abbott, an imprisoned writer who, having been pardoned and released, committed another serious violent crime.

10 *Punishment: Selected Readings*, ed. J. Feinberg and H. Gross (Encino and Belmont: Dickenson, 1975), p. 123.

11 E. Canetti, *Crowds and Power*, trans. C. Stewart (London: Victor Gollancz, 1962), p. 232.

12 Ibid., p. 470.

13 Ibid., p. 424.

Index